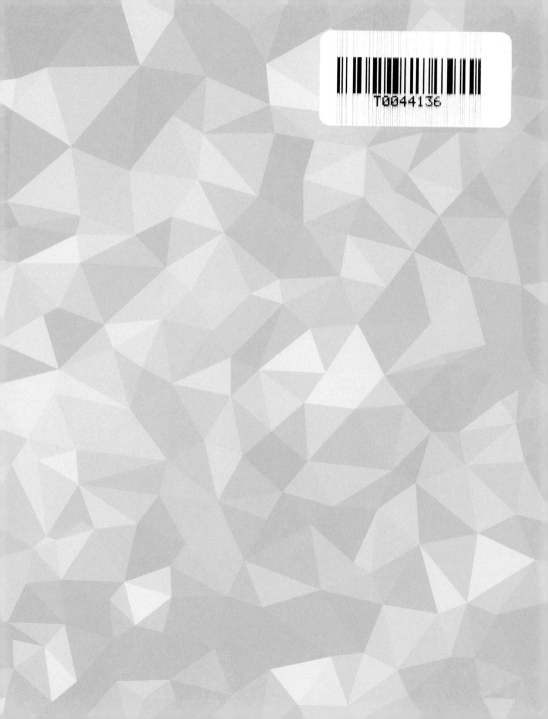

STEPH
CURRY

STEPH CURRY

LIFE LESSONS FROM A LEGEND

SEAN DEVENEY

CASTLE POINT BOOKS
NEW YORK

For Maisie,
my favorite life lesson.
—S.D.

The Castle Point Books trademark is owned by Castle Point Publishing, LLC.
Castle Point books are published and distributed by St. Martin's Publishing Group.

ISBN 978-1-250-28794-6 (paper over board)
ISBN 978-1-250-28815-8 (ebook)

Design by Katie Jennings Campbell
Composition by Noora Cox
Illustrations by Gilang Bogy
Edited by Aimee Chase

Our books may be purchased in bulk for promotional, educational, or business use.

Please contact your local bookseller or the Macmillan Corporate and Premium
Sales Department at 1-800-221-7945, extension 5442,
or by email at MacmillanSpecialMarkets@macmillan.com.

First Edition: 2023

10 9 8 7 6 5 4 3 2

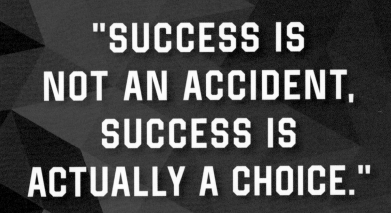

CONTENTS

INTRODUCTION

For Stephen Curry, none of it was preordained—not the MVP awards, not the championship rings, not the scoring titles, not the endorsement deals. Where so many of the world's top athletes are blessed with otherworldly physical qualities, Curry was never so gifted. He is not fast. He is not the muscular type. At 6-foot-2, he is not even tall. When his fourteenth season in the NBA opened, Curry was tied for 432nd in the league in height, out of 482 players.

Curry was not supposed to be an NBA star. It was something he heard from scouts and coaches, over and over. "'Not tall enough,' they said. 'Not strong enough,' they said. 'Won't be able to guard bigger, stronger players at the next level,' they said. When it came to the doubters, there were many," Curry said.

Curry did come from an athletic background. He was the son of Dell Curry, a 16-year NBA veteran and one of the best shooters of his era, who was 6-foot-4 and a sturdy 190 pounds. His mother, Sonya, had been a volleyball player at sports powerhouse Virginia Tech, where Dell Curry also had played.

His parents' genes did not make Stephen Curry a phenom, however. Even as a teenager, when scouts took notice of collegiate prospects, Curry was a good scorer but considered too small to be a big-time prospect. Though he went to high school in Charlotte, surrounded by hoops stalwarts like Duke and North Carolina, recruiters were scarce.

"I wasn't highly touted as a high school prospect," Curry said. "I had nobody really running, knocking on my door saying please, please, please come play for our school." He landed at tiny Davidson College (student body size: fewer than 2,000), the first school to recruit him and just one of three to offer him a scholarship. There, everything changed, particularly as he led the Wildcats to the 2008 Elite Eight with jaw-dropping shooting displays.

Curry easily captured the basketball world's imagination. As much as Curry's slight size held him back early in life, it fueled his popularity during his career rise. It is difficult for most fans to relate to the super-athletic 7-footers who dominate NBA courts, but watching Curry, almost everyone can identify with him because they see something they recognize:

"I'm them. I can't jump the highest. I'm obviously not the biggest, not the strongest. And so they see me out there and I look like a normal person."

What few of his fans see is Curry's not-so-normal dedication to improving his game. After practices, and sometimes before, Curry works through a series of intense drills that combine shooting and running, sprinting from one end of the court to the other and back, constantly shooting. He has been known to hoist 1,000 practice 3-pointers, every day. "Stephen does every drill like his hair is on fire," his trainer, Brandon Payne, said.

Curry is among the best-conditioned players in the NBA, and rarely gets fatigued—he never loses focus during games, which helps him maintain his consistency even when shooting from long distances. No player in his era has changed the game like he has. He cannot dunk or blow past defenders the way other stars can, but he learned early on that he could have an enormous impact by becoming an elite shooter. That was thanks to a simple realization he made early in his career: "Three," Curry explained with a smile, "is always better than two."

For most of its existence, the 3-point shot was viewed as a gimmick, far less reliable than 2-pointers taken close to the basket. Curry challenged that view, though, and revolutionized the way NBA players shoot. The 3-pointer has become the defining offensive staple of this era, and Curry has pushed the shot's boundaries, often pulling up to shoot from five or six feet behind the arc, which is 23 feet, nine inches from the basket. Curry sometimes shoots

STAT ⚡ Curry has dominated the NBA's 3-point record books. He broke Hall of Fame guard Ray Allen's career record (2,973) for 3-pointers made in 2021, and holds the all-time record for most 3-pointers in a season, at 402. In fact, four of the five most prolific 3-point seasons in league history were posted by Curry.

from so far away that he is standing on the center-court logo, which paved the way for the term, "logo shot."

Despite his shooting success, there were lingering doubters

who said Curry would never turn the Warriors into a playoff power because jump-shooters could not thrive in the rough-and-tumble NBA postseason. After four championships and a Finals MVP, Curry and Golden State laid that outlook to rest.

Some people in Curry's shoes might be tempted to thumb a nose at their detractors. Curry never approached his mission that way, though. Instead of focusing on negative voices, Curry set out to show his toughest critic— himself—the positives of what he could achieve.

Stephen Curry was not physically advantaged like most top-level stars in sports. But he will be known as one of the greatest players in league history anyway. How he managed that is a story of hard work and perseverance, of humility and self-sacrifice, of opportunities converted, and a committed focus on what matters most in life.

"I HAVE A LOT TO ACCOMPLISH. I DON'T HAVE ANYTHING TO PROVE."

STAY GROUNDED

Stephen Curry grew up lucky, and not just because, as the son of a respected NBA player, he had few material wants. He was lucky because he grew up around adept teachers who could show him different ways of approaching both his passion—basketball—and himself. He was lucky, too, because he grew up with enough humility to understand the value of learning from those teachers.

His lessons started at home. Dell Curry, his dad, could teach him plenty about the hard work needed to become an exemplary basketball player while his mother, Sonya Curry, could teach him plenty about becoming an exemplary person. Despite the success Dell received on the court, Sonya kept her family humble and grounded. His mother knew how to make sure her son stayed right-sized, and Stephen Curry paid attention.

There were times in high school when Curry put up stellar personal stats but found Sonya annoyed later because she found a flaw in his effort on defense:

"WHENEVER I LEAVE THE HOUSE AND GET READY FOR MY DAY, I KNOW WHAT I'M ABOUT."

"She would be right there on the sidelines yelling. I can make all the shots in the world, but if I let my man score, she would be all over me after the game. I'd score 30, and she would be like, 'You had a horrible game because you didn't play defense.'"

Curry leans on the lessons of his childhood, and the inner stability his parents gave him.

In a message to both, he later said, "The calmness I have in myself is because of y'all."

LEARN FROM YOUR LOVED ONES

When Stephen Curry was in middle school at Queensway Christian, he could not wait to play his first basketball game for his new team. He was the third-smallest player, but he was an obviously talented scorer, often netting 40 points in a game.

PERMANENT REMINDERS

Some of Curry's tattoos include his personal and professional mantras. He has the letters "TCC" tattooed above the number 30 on his left wrist, which dates back to his days at Davidson—"Trust, Commitment, Care," was a mantra of his coach, and 30 was (and remains) his uniform number. He also has the word "WOE" on his right bicep. It stands for "Working on Excellence."

"I REMEMBER WHERE I STARTED AND JUST THE WHOLE JOURNEY. YOU REMIND YOURSELF OF THAT EVERY DAY."

Nothing could keep him from opening night. Except for one thing: Sonya Curry. Just before the big game, young Stephen Curry had neglected to do the dishes, which was his chore that day.

"Four dirty dish plates in the sink, and I didn't get it done," Curry recalled.

If he thought his mother would overlook those dishes and let him go play, Curry quickly learned he was wrong. When he reported to school for the game, he had to inform his team he would not be able to play that day because he had neglected his chores and made his mom mad. The team managed to win, and went undefeated that year, but the memory of that day stayed with Curry:

"That's a pretty embarrassing moment if you go to your first middle school game and you have to tell your team, 'Hey, fellas, I can't play tonight I didn't do the dishes at home.' They're like, 'What? What are you talking about?' Just that lesson taught me there is more to life than basketball."

It was more than a decade later, after he had become a global icon of the game, that Curry brought up the story of his mother and the dishes. The lesson stuck with him, and as a father, he brought it to his own family. At times, Curry can be singularly focused on basketball, and with all the success and accolades he has accumulated during his career, he could hardly be blamed for developing an outsized ego. But that never happened. His family—first his parents, then his wife, Ayesha, whom he met when they were teenagers in Charlotte, and their three children—never let his own opinion of himself get out of control. His mother summed it up in advice she gave him when his career started: "People will love you if you love them," she said. "Give them your all on the court and be nice when you go to the grocery store."

For Curry, that balance between his dazzling work on the court with millions watching and the mundane responsibilities at home for his family keeps him level-headed:

"Every day, just try to stay as grounded as possible. That's how I like to start my days. That's why I love my family so much because they don't let me get a big head at all. They keep it real with me."

"I KNEW MY DAD WAS IN THE NBA AND MADE SOME MONEY BUT EVERYTHING WE GOT, WE HAD TO WORK FOR."

REMEMBER WHERE YOU CAME FROM

Before he was old enough to process what his father did for a living, Curry had fallen in love with basketball. It started with an old hoop erected by his paternal grandfather, Jack, in the yard of his grandparents' home outside Charlottesville, Virginia, the same hoop Dell once used to hone his shot as a kid. As a two-year-old, even before he was able to toddle his way toward that basket, Curry was working on his game using a Fisher Price hoop in the living room of his grandmother, Juanita (the family knew her as "Duckie"). His grandmother would sit in her favorite chair near the television, where she religiously watched Atlanta Braves games, and play the role of Curry's personal announcer:

"She used to be my commentator. She used to be (Warriors broadcaster) Bob Fitzgerald for me, counting down the scores. I'd hit a game-winning shot or whatever, and I'd stumble over and give her a high five and stuff like that."

Curry recounted his exploits in front of Duckie in 2015 as he was accepting his place in history—he had been awarded the league's MVP award, just the sixth point guard to be given that honor. It is a theme that repeats throughout Curry's career. No matter how momentous the individual accomplishment, Curry always ties it back to something foundational from his youth, something he recognizes as critical to his later success.

LOOK BACK WITH GRATITUDE

Very often, Curry will look back to the rickety hoop behind his grandparents' house, hung on a wooden utility pole next to a dirt court pocked with tire tracks and rocks. The well-worn surface at Duckie's taught him to handle the ball with care—the court's undulations could send an errant dribble bouncing out of bounds— and the unstable backboard forced shooting accuracy, just as it had done for his father as well as his brother, Seth, also an excellent NBA shooter.

When he dazzles a defender with an adept move into the lane to set up an easy shot, or when he goes on a hot streak from the 3-point line, Curry knows he owes something to his grandfather, who set up that hoop but died before he got to see Curry use it. "I always felt like the love and the lessons of that hoop got passed down to me," Curry said.

BE TEACHABLE

For the most part, Dell Curry tried to avoid playing the role of the overbearing father to his oldest son. He did not push Stephen into basketball, did not force him to participate in high-level camps or private coaching sessions. He did not need to force his son into that level of training. Stephen wanted it on his own.

When Curry was 15, though, his father recognized a problem. If Steph was serious about his pursuit of basketball, he would need to overhaul the way he shot. Because he was undersized, Curry did not have the strength to shoot a standard jumper, and instead developed a "catapult" style that was easy for defenders to block. By his sophomore year, Curry was 5-feet-8 and 150 pounds, still rail thin and reliant on his awkward catapult shooting motion, but he was strong enough and ready, in his father's opinion, to adopt a more standard shooting approach.

For three months, Dell Curry pulled Steph away from playing competitive basketball to teach him how to shoot like an NBA star, with his hands high in front of him and poised for a quick release. It was essential, according to Curry's dad, to progress slowly, starting with weeks of short shots near the basket. The process was so frustrating and painstaking that Curry would cry as he shot. Stephen's aunt, Jackie Curry, called it, "the summer of tears."

"I was always the smallest kid on my team. I had a terrible, ugly, catapult shot from the time I was 14 because I wasn't strong enough to shoot over my head, and I had to reconstruct that over the summer and it was the worst three months of my life."

His father's resume as a shooter, though, was unquestioned (Dell Curry led the NBA in 3-point shooting, at 47.6%, in 1998–99) and Curry bucked up and cried his way through those three months. He returned to his high school team with the makings of the picture-perfect form for which he became famous. From that experience, Curry learned to lean on those who could teach him, and has developed solid relationships with his coaches at every level.

When giving out credit for his success, Curry goes back not only to his parents but also to his high school coach at Charlotte Christian, Shonn Brown, and his coach at Davidson, Bob McKillop. Along the way, he has developed deep bonds with Warriors trainers and behind-the-scenes assistant coaches:

"It's all a part of the process of taking bits and pieces from different personalities and characters that you come across. It's not one specific person individually that takes all the credit. You learn every single day, be coachable, and just find different ways to challenge yourself and get better."

LIFE LESSONS FROM A LEGEND

- **KEEP YOUR EGO IN CHECK.**
- **HONOR YOUR FAMILY AND YOUR RESPONSIBILITIES.**
- **FIND YOUR SPECIALTY; DEVELOP YOUR EDGE.**
- **SOMETIMES PAIN IS THE ONLY ROAD TO PROGRESS.**
- **EVERY DAY IS A CHANCE TO LEARN AND DO BETTER.**

EMBRACE YOUR UNIQUE JOURNEY

In 2001, Steph Curry was 13 years old and playing in an AAU tournament in Tennessee. His team reached the tournament final, but with the championship on the line, he did not play well, and his team lost. After the game, Curry returned to the hotel with the rest of his team feeling disappointed and depressed. He had already established a goal of playing in the NBA like his father, who was playing for the Toronto Raptors at the time, but here he was, unable to hold his own against his fellow teenagers. With that lofty goal in his head and his inadequate performance at the tournament, the NBA seemed so far off that Curry was starting to give up on his dream.

That's when his parents sat him down and gave him a talk that made an impact. It was not a pep talk. It was more honest, a reality check. Maybe he would get to the NBA, maybe not, his mother told

"KIDS WERE A LOT TALLER, STRONGER, FASTER THAN ME—AND I JUST REALLY COULDN'T KEEP UP."

him. Maybe he would give up on pro basketball at that moment, and that would be fine with his parents. What would not be fine, he was told, was the notion that he was going to let that AAU loss, along with the coaches and scouts who doubted his ability, make the decision for him.

Curry later paraphrased his mother's soliloquy, and it went something like:

"NO ONE gets to write your story but you. Not some scouts. Not some tournament. Not these other kids, who might do this better or that better. And not EVER your last name. None of those people, and none of those things, gets to be the author of your story. Just you. So, think real hard about it. Take your time. And then you go and write what you want to write. But just know that this story—it's yours."

After that, Curry stopped playing AAU basketball, the primary showcase for college coaches looking for players, and focused on his high school career at Charlotte Christian. AAU stressed pure physical prowess over practice time and skill work, and Curry could not keep pace. He was just not big enough. It was in his best interest to work on his shooting and ball handling at Charlotte Christian:

"A lot of it was because I was such a late bloomer—physically, I could not keep up. In AAU, if you're fastest, strongest, tallest, you're probably going to shine. The skilled guys don't necessarily get highlighted like that at that level. It wasn't doing me any good, to get out there and get bulldozed every game. So, those three years, I got to work on my game."

For those next few years, Curry's development took place out of the view of scouts from major basketball colleges. He was within 200 miles of top-tier programs like Duke, North Carolina, and Wake Forest, but because he was not playing AAU, he went unnoticed. If he was not on the radar of college scouts, he was not even in the same galaxy as NBA evaluators.

After taking his mother's guidance into consideration, though, Curry was comfortable with his chosen path.

SHARPEN YOUR TOOLS

The first interaction that Bob McKillop, the longtime head coach at tiny Davidson College, had with Steph Curry had nothing to do with basketball. It was baseball that brought the two together. When Curry was 10, he was the center fielder for his Charlotte-area AAU team, and McKillop's son, Brendan, was his teammate. McKillop watched Curry help lead the team to the North Carolina state

"GOD GIVES YOU WHAT'S FOR YOU, AND YOU'VE GOT TO WALK IN THAT."

championship, and took notice. He thought Curry had a bright future—on the diamond. "He'd have a shot at the majors if he had focused on baseball," McKillop later commented.

Fortunately for McKillop, basketball was Curry's greatest love. Also fortunate for McKillop was the connection he made with the Curry family during those baseball weekends, which allowed him to keep a closer eye on Steph's development as a basketball player. While Curry went unnoticed by most Division I schools, Davidson coaches were a steady presence at his Charlotte Christian games. Being ranked No. 300 in the country on the recruiting chart meant that Curry didn't receive a flood of collegiate offers. Even Virginia Tech, the alma mater of both Dell and Sonya Curry, offered him little more than an invitation to try out as a walk-on.

When McKillop sat down with the Currys to offer Steph a scholarship, Steph eagerly accepted. Knowing that his wispy build was an impediment, Sonya promised she would "fatten up" her son before he arrived on campus. No need, McKillop assured her. He did not want anything interfering with Curry's top weapon: his shot. "We'll take him just as he is," McKillop told her. That was fortunate, because Curry showed up at Davidson with the same wispy build he'd had when he was recruited.

Being at a small school helped Curry keep his ego in check. He still harbored big NBA dreams, but playing for a college where the basketball team was forced to share a practice court with the volleyball team served as a consistent reminder to Curry that his path to his dream was still being forged:

"I NEVER DRANK MY OWN KOOL-AID."

"I NEVER GOT TOO AHEAD OF MYSELF IN TERMS OF JOURNEY."

"There was always an acknowledgment of the value everybody brought to the table to help me be successful. I know for a fact I'm not playing without every single person I got to rock with on the floor, so I carried that to the league. But you know, those lessons of how you build success and being in the moment came from Davidson."

"Going to Davidson, and playing—and winning—at that level of hoops . . . it made me who I am, in a way. It made me understand what it means to build something. Like, truly build something. Something that no one can ever take away from you. Something that's all your own."

FORTIFY YOUR CONFIDENCE, EVEN IN HARD TIMES

Winning at Davidson, too, was special for Curry in a way that winning at a collegiate powerhouse would not have been. In retrospect, Curry deserved a spot at a school like Duke or North Carolina, Kansas or Kentucky. But it's unclear whether he would be the Stephen Curry the world knows now if he had:

One game into his college career, it didn't appear that Curry and the Wildcats would be unstoppable. Facing Eastern Michigan in Ann Arbor, Davidson trailed by 16 points at halftime and had to rally in the second half to win. Curry's debut was inauspicious. He had an eye-popping 13 turnovers in the game (nine in the first half) and shot

5-for-12 from the field, missing two of his four free throws.

McKillop stuck with his prized freshman, though, and Curry bounced back with 32 points and nine rebounds against Michigan the next night:

> *"That was all just Coach McKillop seeing the long game. He could have sat me down after that first half. But he let me play through my mistakes. . . . Thirteen turnovers, first game. I got to play right away. I had to work through that and not lose confidence in myself. I got to reap the benefits of that later on."*

Davidson went 29-5 and won the Southern Conference championship in Curry's first year, losing to Syracuse in the first round of the NCAA tournament. Curry was eighth in the nation in points (730) and third in 3-pointers (122), but still largely went overlooked because he played for such a small school. It was as a sophomore, though, that Curry's legend began to take shape.

It began with adversity: The Wildcats opened the season just 4-6, but three of the losses were against top 10 teams (North Carolina, Duke, and UCLA). Curry averaged only 19.7 points in those three games, more than 6 points lower than what his season average would be. He shot terribly, making 41.4% of his attempts from the field and 31% from the 3-point line in those first 10 games. The rest of the team played well—they lost by only 4 points to UNC and by 6 to Duke— but Curry felt he was shortchanging them with his poor showing.

There was some question, too, about whether Curry should play at all. He had suffered a wrist injury that would require surgery to fix, and had the option of either taking the rest of the year off or taping up the wrist and playing through it. He did not want to let his team down. He played, even as he struggled. Curry could not see it at the time, but those losses were critical in toughening him up for the wins that were to come.

TURN IT AROUND
DESPITE THE ODDS

By the end of the season, Curry's tools were plenty sharp. Davidson again won the Southern Conference in 2008 and entered the NCAA tournament on a 22-game winning streak, though many of those wins were against other mid-major Southern Conference schools. Their opening matchup looked daunting: Gonzaga, ranked No. 24 in the nation.

But this is where Curry's rise as a basketball star began. He knocked down eight of his ten 3-point attempts and tallied 40 points to fuel an upset over Gonzaga, and did not stop there. He followed that with 30 points in another upset, over No. 8 Georgetown, and 33 points in a Sweet 16 win over Wisconsin (which had been No. 6 in the nation).

It was not until the Elite Eight that Davidson's run was defused, in a 2-point loss to No. 4 Kansas, a team that featured seven future NBA players, including future champion Mario Chalmers and Curry's teammate-to-be with the Warriors, Brandon Rush. They would go on to win the national championship, but Curry had 25 points in the game.

In the span of 10 days, Curry had emerged from a rough start to the season to become a household name. He would earn a spot on the All-American team, and be invited to that year's Espy Awards in Los Angeles as a contender for Best Breakout Performance. Even after the loss to Kansas, Curry's prospects changed, and he started seeing options that weren't there before:

"The crazy thing is right after the game, I honestly hadn't thought about the NBA or the draft or anything like that. First question I got in the locker room after the game was, 'Are you declaring for the draft?' I looked at the reporter like he was an idiot. I'd never thought of it. In my mind, I was never making that jump at that point."

STAT ⚡ In his sophomore season, Curry set an NCAA record by making 162 3-pointers in a season. He shot 41.2% from the 3-point line in his career, and despite playing only three seasons, he holds the Southern Conference record for 3-pointers made (414).

Curry kept his NBA dream in his pocket. He was not going to move forward with it right then, after his sophomore season, even as scouts and talent evaluators began pegging him as a first-round draft pick, virtually guaranteeing him a spot in the league. He did not feel the need to hurry, though top draft spots were rarely used on players who spent more than two years in college. For Curry, the NBA would always be there. He was working on his own timeline. He was writing his own story, his own way.

Not getting the attention he wanted right away, in high school and in college, was actually a benefit to Curry. "It taught me patience," Curry said. "It taught me to appreciate the opportunity you have, and that everything happens for a reason, and to embrace whatever your story is. And the rest is history."

"MAKE SURE YOU KNOW WHAT JOURNEY YOU ARE ON, AND WHAT YOUR PACE IS."

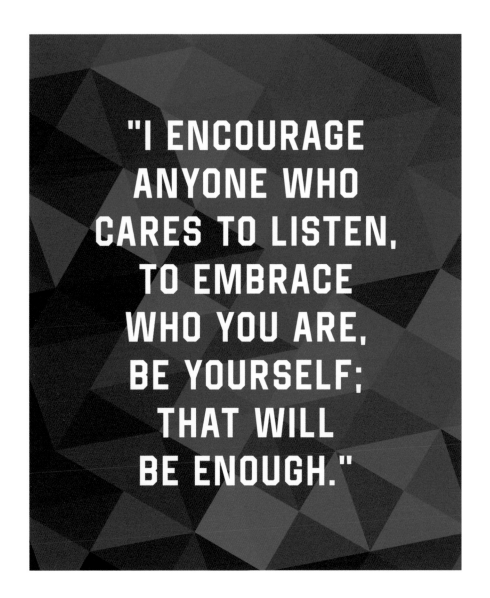

"I ENCOURAGE
ANYONE WHO
CARES TO LISTEN,
TO EMBRACE
WHO YOU ARE,
BE YOURSELF;
THAT WILL
BE ENOUGH."

DON'T ACT LIKE YOU'RE BETTER

The effect Curry has on those around him is unique. Former Warriors teammate Andrew Bogut, who spent 14 seasons in the NBA playing for four franchises, was asked about playing alongside Curry, and he minced no words in his response. Sure, Curry is a great player. But Bogut focused on something else: "He is one of the few superstars I have been around that *does not* act like a superstar. He is one of the best human beings in the NBA."

That is another aspect of Curry's story that remains mostly his alone. Curry is one of the most approachable stars in sports, an active participant in his causes, a magnet for kids, and a favorite of the NBA media and the Warriors staff because of the respect he shows them.

Curry intentionally tries to sidestep the drama that usually attends a life of fame and fortune. Not only does that lead him to be happier, but it also leaves an impact on those around him:

> *"I'm truly proud of that in terms of all the variables that play out, you know, even different*

stereotypes within the NBA and how people see athletes in general, trying to break that—which is being myself."

NEVER LOSE YOUR CHIP

Even with his success in college and the NBA success that followed, Curry has never lost sight of the fact that he was readily overlooked when he was coming up through the ranks. There is a word he clings to more than any other when he needs a jolt of energy, when he needs reminding of just how unorthodox his journey had to be: underrated.

That word, for him, holds the key to his unwavering confidence in himself. A documentary that came out in 2023 about his life and rise in basketball is titled *Underrated*. He started a tour for high school players—in both basketball and in golf, his second love—called the "Underrated Tour."

"Underrated" is the word that rings in his ears every time he works on his game.

METEORIC RISE

When Curry got back from the first weekend of the 2008 NCAA tournament, he logged into his Facebook page, and found that under Friend Requests there was an infinity sign. "My computer crashed," Curry said. "I was thinking, I don't even know how to handle this."

Being underrated defined those early years as a young player who almost gave up on basketball. He does not hide from that, though, even as he boasts one of the greatest NBA resumes of all time. Yes, he was a self-described "scrawny" kid all the way into college. Yes, he was ranked No. 300 nationally as a prospect. Yes, he wound up at Davidson because no one else wanted him.

Curry doesn't hide that humbling ride to fame; he clings to it.

"People assume that, once you've started to have a certain amount of success, 'feeling underrated' starts going away," Curry said. "And that, once you've finally reached any sort of ultimate goal . . . it starts going away forever. But from my own experience? In your head, honestly—it never goes away. In mine, it's never even diminished."

Curry's unique story is a key component of his success. He has taken the underrated label and turned

"ME BEING A THREE-STAR RECRUIT, NOT EVEN CRACKING THE TOP 200 IN THE STATE, ALL THAT STILL IS MOTIVATION."

> ## "IF YOU FIGURE OUT HOW TO HARNESS [FEELING UNDERRATED], IT CAN BECOME A FEELING THAT YOU IMPOSE ON THE WORLD."

it around, thrived on it, and finds ways to use his former weaknesses as advantages. He will never lose the chip on the shoulder he developed from all those years when very few people believed in him. Now it's clear to the whole world that whoever was doing the rating got it wrong. Curry wants to leave no doubt as to just how wrong they were, and he finds power in that.

LIFE LESSONS FROM A LEGEND

- THERE IS MORE THAN ONE PATH TO EVERY GOAL.
- DON'T LET A BAD SITUATION HOLD YOU BACK.
- LET YOUR STORY UNFOLD AT ITS OWN PACE.
- KEEP YOUR EDGE, AND LET IT MOTIVATE YOU.

LET ADVERSITY BE YOUR GUIDE

CHAPTER 3

Stephen Curry was hopeful. It was a warm Thursday in June 2009, and he was in New York City, where he would be selected in that year's NBA Draft. He was sure of that, but not of much else.

He had returned to Davidson for his junior season, and had a successful run, leading the nation in scoring (28.6 points per game) while averaging 5.5 assists and making 130 3-pointers, fifth in all of college basketball. The Wildcats had not recaptured their NCAA tournament magic, failing to qualify despite a 26-7 record after they were ousted by Charleston in the Southern Conference championship.

Curry was perhaps the most divisive player in his draft class when it came to popular opinion—there were those who were certain he could bring his collegiate success to the

NBA, and those who were sure his lack of size and speed would limit what he could accomplish.

One draft commentator, former Oklahoma State star Doug Gottlieb, was in the latter camp. He sent out a tweet that Curry has held onto his entire career: "He doesn't have the upside of (Ricky) Rubio. (Brandon) Jennings, (Jonny) Flynn, (Patty) Mills, (Jeff) Teague all more athletic."

EXPECT SOME TWISTS AND TURNS

Curry had shown enough, though, to be considered one of the Top 10 prospects in the draft, and knew for certain that he would land in the draft's Top 8. That's because the eighth pick was held by the New York Knicks, and the team had made it clear that they coveted Curry: "We wanted him so bad, I could taste it," coach Mike D'Antoni later said.

The feeling was mutual. Curry had an excellent pre-draft workout with D'Antoni, who had previously coached Curry's point-guard hero, Steve Nash, in Phoenix. It was all

lined up: The Knicks needed a point guard, and they wanted a star. Curry needed a big stage, and playing nightly at Madison Square Garden is as big as it gets.

Watching the picks come off the board, Curry's nerves were increasingly tense. The draft came to Minnesota, which had Nos. 5 and 6. It seemed almost impossible that the Timberwolves could have two picks and not take a shot on Curry. He figured it was down to the bright lights of Manhattan or the frigid winters of the Upper Midwest.

The Timberwolves took a point guard at No. 5, Rubio, the Spanish phenom, and another point guard after that, Syracuse's Flynn. "It was like, 'That's weird. What's the plan there? Why am I still sitting here?'" Curry said.

Curry was not going to Minnesota. He would be going to New York, as long as the Warriors passed on him. Curry had declined to work out for Golden State, sending the Warriors the message that he did not want to be there. If that was not clear enough, Curry's agent sent the Warriors' front office a text on draft night: "Please don't pick Steph."

Except the Warriors did not follow the script. General manager Larry Riley had become enamored with Curry during his junior season. The Warriors picked Curry. Sonya Curry froze: "I was stomach punched," she said.

Steph Curry was baffled, too. "I was a little shocked, to be sure," he said. "When I heard my name, my first thought was, 'Wait, that's not the Knicks.'"

EMBRACE EVERY OPPORTUNITY

Shortly after he was picked, Curry could be seen walking through a back tunnel at Madison Square Garden chanting "Golden State, Golden State, Golden State." Later, he confessed: "To be honest, I didn't even know where Golden State played. I had no clue."

What he did know was that there were reasons to keep him away from the Warriors: The franchise was a mess, with a very unpopular owner named Chris Cohan (who was known more for his excessive litigiousness than for his love of the team or its players), and just one playoff appearance dating back to 1994.

"Um, what's the word? Turmoil?" Stephen Curry said, describing the state of the Warriors at the time. Even at that young age, though, Curry was blessed with perspective. He was not going to be a Knick, but

"THERE IS ALWAYS A LESSON TO LEARN."

he had much to celebrate. He was now officially in the NBA—not bad for an AAU outcast, ranked No. 300 nationally, who was barely able to get a Division I college offer. He was quick to accept becoming a Warrior, with his gratitude overshadowing his disappointment.

From the moment the Warriors drafted Curry, the question of how his dynamic with Monta Ellis, the team's incumbent star point guard, would work lingered over the team. Concerns about turmoil in Golden State hung over the Curry family as Steph set off across the country, and their concerns did not take long to materialize.

When the Warriors gathered for the annual media day event—the very first time reporters have full access to players—to start training camp in 2009, Ellis finally spoke on the subject of the pairing with Curry.

It did not go well.

If the Warriors planned to play Ellis and Curry together, Ellis foresaw trouble. "Can't. We just can't," Ellis said. "Not going to win that way. Can't do it." The comments opened up more cracks within the team, all of which were starting to show.

"It was weird," Curry said, describing Ellis's frigid welcome to the team. "Thankfully I had people in my ear talking about all [Ellis] had been through. But it was a rude awakening, to be sure."

At another media day table, the franchise's veteran leader, Stephen Jackson, was telling reporters he wanted a trade out of Golden State.

Those were the highlights of Curry's first official day of NBA work. Turmoil, indeed.

LOOK FOR THE GOOD IN OTHERS

The trouble was, that discontent and infighting was all too common with the Warriors:

> *"They were in a period where, from ownership on down, you can talk about corporate culture and the environment you have to go into work in every day, it was all*

bad. That filtered through
everything we did. That was what
I walked in as a twenty-one-year-
old, bright-eyed rookie."

But, looking back, Curry could see where the Warriors could have encouraged more solidarity. They had not done enough to respect that Ellis had his own story, his own journey into the NBA—he grew up poor in Mississippi and skipped college to enter the NBA Draft. He was not highly rated, and fell into the second round on draft night. But he scratched his way to a spot in the league, and had risen to stardom with the Warriors. To select Curry without sitting down with Ellis to outline how the pairing could work and to get his input left Ellis feeling isolated.

Curry had the perspective to avoid taking Ellis' attitude personally and focused on what Ellis brought to the team:

"The thing everyone talks about is
what he said at training camp my
rookie year. That was how our
relationship started. But his

talent, the way he had the mindset
of, 'Give me the ball, I am going to
get you all a bucket,' and he did. He
was unbelievable. Monta doesn't
get enough credit for his journey."

Curry does not remember Ellis for the awkward comments on Media Day. Instead, he remembers a point early in his career in which he was struggling to make shots, over about a two-week span. Ellis, who was naturally quiet and proud, had maintained a cool distance from Curry, who was also naturally quiet and proud.

During his slump, though, it was obvious that Curry was frustrated. After practice one day, his phone rang.

It was Ellis:

"He just gave me some good words
of encouragement. He did not have
to do that, nobody has to do that,
especially with the storyline that
there was a threat between us. He
didn't care, it was just about, how
do we get better together and get
to know each other? You're dealing

"WE WERE KIND OF IN A LITTLE CHAOTIC STATE AS A TEAM."

with pressure and expectations, and I am dealing with the same stuff. We couldn't be more different in our journeys to get to the league, but that was a good connection. I love Monta for that."

The pairing of Ellis and Curry created adversity for the Warriors on the court. But the simple act of Ellis offering his help to Curry off the court helped smooth out that rough spot.

ACCEPT HELP

On November 17, 2009, Curry had just wrapped up his tenth game in the NBA, a loss in Cleveland that dropped the wayward Warriors to 3-7. The previous day, Golden State had finally granted Jackson his wish and traded him to Charlotte, leaving a void in veteran leadership on what felt like an increasingly rudderless team.

Curry notched 14 points, while the Cavs were led by the league's biggest young star, LeBron James, who scored 31. James had taken an interest in Curry dating back to the 2008 tournament run, when he showed up at Ford Field in Detroit to watch Davidson trounce Wisconsin in the Sweet 16, and had gone to see Curry play in Charlotte the next season.

After the game, James tracked down Curry and pulled him aside. The Warriors were a mess and James could relate, because the

"I WAS JUST TRYING TO FIND MY WAY."

Cavaliers were 35-47 in James' first year and fired their coach in his second year.

Curry was rapt. During James' visit to Charlotte in 2009, he had given Curry an autographed jersey with the tagline, "To the King of Basketball in North Carolina," and Curry still had it hanging on the wall at his childhood home back in Charlotte. Now, James was offering advice on NBA survival.

"The one thing that you can control is your energy, effort, and focus on getting better every single day," Curry remembered James saying. "Then just try to find a way to become your style of a leader. He said you'll last a lot of years in this league if that is the one thing that you focus on."

Not long after that, Curry and the Warriors faced the Lakers and another of the top players in the league, star guard Kobe Bryant. The Lakers won easily, but Curry had a move during the game in which he followed up a 3-pointer with a nifty spin move and a make off the backboard. He did not know it until he saw highlights after the game, but Bryant leaned over to Lakers teammate Robert Scare and could be seen to say, "That [expletive] is nice!"

"LIFE WILL TEACH YOU EVERYTHING YOU NEED TO LEARN AND KNOW— YOU JUST HAVE TO BE OPEN TO WHAT THOSE LESSONS ARE."

"WHEN YOU ARE AROUND GREATNESS, IT JUST ENCOURAGES YOU AND MOTIVATES YOU."

"You don't know how much confidence that gave me," Curry said. "I thought, I am the best player in the world now!"

Bryant, too, would be a source of help for Curry throughout his early NBA career. He advised Curry to be willing to alter his nice-guy demeanor with his teammates when necessary.

"He didn't care if his teammates liked him in the moment. If he got on them, if he yelled at them, or whatever, he expected greatness from them."

Early in his career, Curry soaked up lessons wherever he could get them, but when they came from players on the level of James and Bryant, they carried extra weight.

STAY POSITIVE

It was May 2011, and Bob Myers was only a month into his job as Warriors assistant general manager, sitting nervously in a doctor's office in the Bay Area with Steph Curry, the one player who, he knew, had the potential to carry his new employer to glory.

Only there was a significant obstacle. Curry was having trouble keeping his ankles healthy. The statistics showed that Curry had the talent to be something special, as a scorer (18.6 points in his second season), as a passer (5.8 assists), and, especially, as a perimeter shooter (44.2%). The injuries, though, were holding him back.

Curry was coming off a season in which he suffered a series of injuries that left the ligaments in his ankles torn and scarred. His right ankle had gotten so fragile that he did not need a high-impact event to injure them—he could get hurt simply running up and down the court. He would need surgery. Myers knew that for NBA athletes, especially thinly built 23-year-olds like Curry, ankle problems could derail an entire career.

Myers looked at Curry, the No. 7 pick in the 2009 draft, and could not lose the feeling that there was something unfair about him having to be in this doctor's office, about this onslaught of ankle problems.

Worse, the surgeons could not be certain what would happen once they looked inside Curry's ankle.

There was a chance the problem would require a relatively mild clean-up. Or there was a chance he needed a full ankle reconstruction.

"That was a really scary experience, for sure," Curry said.

Myers agreed: "I remember thinking that day, 'This can't be how his career goes. This isn't how it's supposed to be.'"

Indeed, it was not how Curry's career went. The surgery was a success, and Curry did not need his ankle rebuilt. Afterward, Curry not only had to rehab, he also underwent a complete overhaul of his gait. His feet typically landed too far to the outside, putting excess pressure on the ankles, and his ability to play basketball at a high level depended on changing the very way he walked. That rehab process was one of the most difficult periods of his life:

"I never played with injuries my entire basketball career. . . . Then it just kept happening. I

didn't even have to step on someone's foot or anything, I could just be running on the court and change direction and that joint would flip. It was scary because I did not have any control over the situation."

For Curry, a man of faith, sometimes not being in control is a test. He could not see, in the depths of his rehab, how the ankle injuries would work out for the best in the end. He had to work at staying positive as much as at fixing his ankles:

"Anytime you go into rehab, if you can't stay positive and you can't stay motivated,

if you get into your feelings and all that, it's a lonely and miserable feeling. Thankfully, I was young and naïve enough that I didn't have anything else to worry about except get healthy and let everything take care of itself."

HAVE FAITH IN THE SILVER LINING

The injuries may have actually helped Curry in the long run in a most unusual way. After his third season, he was eligible for a contract extension with the Warriors. At the time, top players in the league were paid in excess of $20 million per season, but with

"DON'T COUNT ANYBODY ELSE'S MONEY."

"I TRIED TO . . . NEVER RENEGOTIATE WITH MYSELF, NEVER SECOND-GUESS, NEVER COME BACK AND SAY I SHOULDA-COULDA-WOULDA."

"AT THE END OF THE DAY, WHEN YOU SIGN, THAT'S YOUR DECISION. YOU ARE GOING TO ROCK WITH IT."

his injuries, Curry was not a top player. After weeks of negotiation, Curry agreed to a contract with the Warriors worth $11 million per season for four seasons.

Because Golden State had a star player earning half what other stars made, the team had the financial wiggle room down the road to re-sign other young stars,

THE KLAY-CURRY CONNECTION

One of the turning points for Curry's Warriors came in 2011, when the team drafted guard Klay Thompson from Washington State, who teamed with Curry to form a backcourt known as the "Splash Brothers." The pair had much in common—both were quiet personalities, both had fathers who had been NBA stars (Mychal Thompson, a 13-year NBA veteran, is Klay's father), and both were excellent shooters. Early in their careers, though, the two kept their distance from one another. They bonded over golf and Sangria on a 2014 trip to Spain for the World Championship and have been close since.

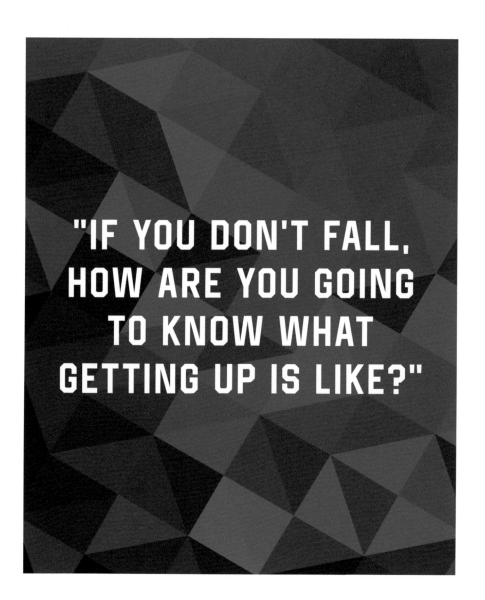

"IF YOU DON'T FALL, HOW ARE YOU GOING TO KNOW WHAT GETTING UP IS LIKE?"

STAT ⚡ In his first three NBA seasons, Curry was only averaging 4.7 3-point shots per game. That changed once he recovered from ankle surgery, and once the Warriors redesigned the team around him. In 2012–13, Curry broke out with 22.9 points and began firing up 3-pointers like no one else in the league: 7.7 per game. That started a streak of six straight seasons leading the league in 3-point attempts.

like Draymond Green and Klay Thompson. They also had the money to acquire key veteran Andre Iguodala and, later, star forward Kevin Durant. Those were all integral to the Warriors' future success.

As soon as he signed the deal, Curry promised himself there would be no regrets, that he would move forward secure in the knowledge that he'd just created a massive amount of wealth for his family, and that he would not look with envy at the paychecks other players were getting.

As he soared into stardom once his ankles healed, Curry became the best bargain in pro sports, and joked that from the Warriors' perspective, the contract was "the most favorable in NBA history." He stuck to his no-regrets vow, though.

And things did work out in his favor. Winning four NBA championships is a significant part of Curry's legacy, but it could be argued that he would not have won those titles without spending a few years as a bargain. He struggled with his ankle rehab in 2011 and 2012, but he maintained his faith that good things were coming his way:

"There is something in my spirit that I knew this wasn't the end of where I was going to go, that I just needed a little bit of breathing room to get healthy."

He *did* finally get healthy in the 2012–13 season, playing 78 games to help the Warriors earn a spot in the playoffs. The next season, Curry was an All-Star. And in 2015, just three years removed from his personal low point, Curry was named the league MVP as the Warriors won their first championship in 40 years.

LIFE LESSONS FROM A LEGEND

- **EVEN IN A BAD SITUATION, YOU CAN KEEP YOUR HEAD DOWN AND WORK ON IMPROVING.**
- **BE WILLING TO ASK FOR HELP AND ABSORB ADVICE.**
- **A NEGATIVE IN THE PRESENT COULD BE A POSITIVE IN THE FUTURE.**

WORK HARD (ER)

CHAPTER 4

When he was a kid, Curry and his cousin would go over to the shopping mall in their Charlotte neighborhood, where one of the stores was of special interest: the GNC nutrition store. They were young and skinny, and they stood out like stalks of celery in the beef case. The boys did not have any money, certainly not enough for a canister of creatine, but they liked the idea that there was a secret miracle powder out there that could cause them to sprout bulbous biceps in a matter of days. "We'd stay in there for twenty minutes, easy," Curry recalled, "staring at these giant tubs of mystery powder, like—*Must . . . have . . . the Wheybolic.*"

If there is anything Curry has learned—and even then, really, he knew it—it's that there is no magic potion that can lead to instant success. There is only one way to attain that success, and that is through a steady and rigorous regimen of hard work. He had seen it from his father, and from the NBA players he got to witness as he was growing up:

"IT'S IN OUR DNA AND OUR BLOOD, LOVING BASKETBALL, WE HAVE BEEN AROUND IT OUR ENTIRE LIFE."

"That work ethic and how to be a true professional in the sense that, every day, there is something that you can pick up. I used to not only watch him but all his teammates."

Along the way, Curry has found that he learned to love the work. Well, *love* is probably too strong a word. He appreciates the work, and thrives on what it allows him to do in game situations. There is chaos in games and in life, but he finds a welcome sense of consistency and reliability in rigorous practice that offsets the unpredictability of games.

"Talent can take you so far, and we all know that," says Curry, "but to develop a real skill around that is the reps, and you have to love it."

MAKE A COMMITMENT

In the midst of his third season, the Warriors were still a team in turmoil. There was a new ownership group in charge, and everyone in that group was determined to drag Golden State out of the ranks of perennial losers. Curry himself missed nearly half the year letting the new ligaments in his ankle heal. After a long run, the team broke up the Curry-Monta Ellis backcourt by trading Ellis to Milwaukee for center Andrew Bogut.

It was a deeply unpopular move for Warriors fans, who mostly had an allegiance to Ellis. New owner Joe Lacob was relentlessly booed by fans after the trade. But what the Warriors fans didn't know was that trading Ellis would unleash Curry, and help him reach his potential.

Curry's coach at the time, former star point guard Mark Jackson, pulled him aside after the trade was made and let Curry know that he was almost traded, too, but that he had stepped in to prevent it. He also wanted to make sure Curry knew that it would now be his team. As Curry remembers it, he said, "I'm going to give you the keys. We really believe in you; we just have to get you healthy, and that's what the rest of the season is going to be about."

Then Jackson gave Curry a solemn look and said, "Don't make me a liar."

Curry was shocked. It was a lot to take on and would be a huge turning point in his NBA career. He would no longer have to operate uncomfortably in Ellis' shadow. Instead, he would be the Warriors' centerpiece.

Curry knew, though, that increased opportunity would mean increased attention from defenses—and increased responsibility to his teammates.

STAT ⚡ Curry's noticeable talent made him a shoe-in for the NBA's MVP for the 2014–15 season. He won by a significant margin. He came back the next season, though, an even better player, as his scoring average leaped from 23.8 points to 30.1, the largest increase for a reigning MVP in league history.

Here was an opportunity for Curry to not only help his own numbers, but to reset the Warriors' whole culture, too. The team had gone 85-155 in his first three NBA seasons, a lowly .354 winning percentage, and it was not for a lack of talent, nor was it all related to injuries and the ownership change. There was a lack of commitment being shown by the players to do their jobs as best as they could.

Few of the Warriors put in extra work, and few seemed all that interested in doing everything they could to make the team function at its best. Curry remembered the

"I DIDN'T REALLY HAVE A VOICE, BUT I KNEW I COULD LEAD BY EXAMPLE."

"I DO PRIDE MYSELF ON TRYING TO BE THE HARDEST WORKER AND THE MOST CONSISTENT WORKER."

advice from LeBron James—keep working on your own game while the franchise figures things out—and quietly set out to do just that.

"I knew every day I was showing up to work to get better, and whether it was in front of people or my teammates saw or management saw, whatever it was, I tried to be as consistent as possible with that. That would set me up for whenever we figured out what our identity was and got a solid roster in place. People could just fall in line and follow that lead and great things would happen."

Curry wanted to see the Warriors defined more by a sense of selflessness and sacrifice, and for him, selflessness manifested itself in his work ethic. Not putting in enough work, in Curry's mind, is letting himself down, letting down all the people who helped his career along the way, and letting down his teammates, who thrive when he is at his peak.

A strong work ethic might be Curry's most important attribute. Even though there were some who knocked Curry down because of his size and skill level, no one

questioned his sense of commitment to basketball. He hoped to bring that level of intensity to his team.

Curry has never been a particularly vocal player, but he figured he could help the Warriors build their commitment to the work and each other, gradually and consistently, by setting the example himself.

> *"My parents and coaches had high expectations. They weren't sure of my eventual success—no one could have been—but they were sure of my commitment. They taught me to give it my all and put everything I had into my game. In team sports, other people rely on you to train your best and try your hardest."*

DON'T SKIP STEPS

On a typical summer afternoon at Accelerate Basketball in Charlotte, you are likely to find Steph Curry on the floor with trainer Brandon Payne. If you stay to watch, you may wonder whether Curry is training for the NBA or the circus.

Curry might be dribbling two basketballs simultaneously while wearing oversized dark glasses that prevent him from relying on his vision. Or you might see Curry dribbling to one side with his right hand while bouncing two tennis balls off a wall with his left. Or you could see Curry trying to maintain a dribble while having powerful strobe lights flashed in his eyes.

No matter what, you'd see Curry running, a lot. And shooting. A typical drill would have Curry shooting a 3-pointer in one corner, sprinting to the opposite corner and firing up another three, then back in a sprint to the other corner, weaving his way around the court as fast as possible in a shot-chucking blur.

Payne and Curry are meticulous in the way the workout is run, careful to stress efficiency of action within a condensed time period instead of engaging in marathon workouts. His training sessions are meant to last about 90 minutes. NBA games run just a bit longer than 90 minutes, and Curry wants his workouts to simulate the intensity of a game, even if the work he's doing is much different:

> *"The curse of society today is everyone sees the finished product, but nobody understands how you got there, what the road map was, the amount of reps it takes to get to that level."*

Curry does not expect perfection from his workouts, but he does strive to get as close as possible, and he ratchets the intensity in stages. Curry does not walk onto the practice floor as Steph Curry, NBA legend. He is just another shooter trying to find a rhythm, starting with 4-footers and working his way out:

> *"The worst thing you can do as a basketball player is to come into the gym and start firing shots up from the 3-point line. You need to warm up and calibrate your mechanics in close to the basket. . . . You want to get those perfect makes on your shots up close because if you are not perfect there, there is no way you're going to be perfect behind that 3-point line or even farther."*

Precision is a key focus in most of his practices. At one point, Curry and Payne used the Noah Shooting system to track not only whether his shot went in, but how close it was to achieving the optimal angle and dropping straight into the net without touching the rim. Anything that rattled against the basket was considered a miss. Curry not only had to make a set number of shots, but he had to swish them.

There is a whiff of insanity around Curry's workouts. Some professional athletes could not

---

STAT ⚡ As part of his shooting regimen, Curry makes 100 3-pointers in a workout—and aims to make them in 110 attempts or fewer.

---

handle them. Payne remembered one prominent unnamed NBA player who went through the first five minutes of a typical sprint-and-shoot session, sat himself on the baseline, his breathing heavy, then went outside and vomited. When they had the No. 2 pick in the 2020 NBA Draft, the Warriors put Anthony Edwards (who was eventually the first overall pick) through one of Curry's workouts, and Edwards admitted he had to jog his way—not sprint, the way Curry does—through the test.

Curry does not advise jumping straight into his workout regimen. The whole process is about gradual fine-tuning:

"It is a step-by-step process," he explains. "There's a lot that goes into it in making sure that you find ways to get better every single day."

In the end, the overall goal is to be able to run, almost nonstop, over the course of a full NBA basketball game, and to do so in every game over a span of as long as eight months. That way, he's prepared if the Warriors play in the league's Finals.

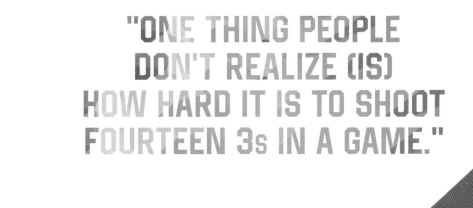

"ONE THING PEOPLE DON'T REALIZE (IS) HOW HARD IT IS TO SHOOT FOURTEEN 3s IN A GAME."

He knows that players look at him, his slight frame and unremarkable athleticism, breaking records and winning NBA championships, and figure they can emulate his game. Maybe, but they will have to walk each step to get there.

"When you see me over here in the gym," says Curry, "don't skip that part. That part is the work."

BUILD FOR THE LONG GAME

At his peak, in 2020–21, Curry attempted an average of 12.7 3-point shots per game. He made 42.1% of them, and led the NBA with 32 points. That season, Curry's top running mate, fellow guard Klay Thompson, was out as he rehabbed from a knee and Achilles tendon injury. The rest of Curry's supporting cast was mostly young and inexperienced. Every night was a challenge.

But Curry has always accepted that the work had to be done, that his game-day successes depended on what he did on the practice floor. That correlates directly to his start in basketball, to his time as an overlooked young prospect wondering where all the recruiters were. Back then, Curry could not gain weight or muscle, and could not turn himself into a No. 1 recruit. He could, however, work on his shot. He could be in top condition.

He accelerated that approach when he got to the NBA and saw that *everyone* was a top-notch athlete. "It was that work ethic, established early on, that set me on the course which has taken me where I am today," Curry said.

Curry's style of play is dependent on his ability to outlast opponents, to wear them down and fight through their attempts to wear him down. He needs quickness and endurance to work around screens and get open, and, just as importantly, he needs enough energy to get his shots off quickly and accurately. When he attacks the basket, Curry relies on deft footwork to get opponents off balance and create space for himself.

"IF I'VE BEEN LUCKY
IN THE NBA, IT'S
BECAUSE OF THOSE
THOUSANDS OF HOURS,
EARLY IN THE MORNING
AND LATE AT NIGHT,
WORKING TO
PROVE MYSELF.
TO PROVE
THEM WRONG."

"IT'S ABOUT
NOT BEING
COMPLACENT AND
ALWAYS TRYING
TO GET BETTER,
NO MATTER
HOW HARD THAT
MISSION MIGHT BE."

"YOU GOTTA BE BUILT FOR THE LONG GAME."

He has honed those key abilities so he can be as sharp at game's end as he is in the opening quarter.

BAN COMPLACENCY

To be sure, Steph Curry is no robot. He is human like the rest of us, with good days and bad. He does not enjoy his workouts, but they're a means to an end. If he had his choice, he probably wouldn't spend every summer afternoon sprinting like a maniac or juggling tennis balls. As Payne explained: "He's in love with getting better. He just has to put up with the process to get there."

And so Payne and Curry use a lot of headspace to come up with ideas for different drills, different challenges to keep Curry engaged and maintain a sense of fun (or, at least, variety). These drills get names that make them sound more like casino games than parts of a workout plan: "Full-Court Star," "21," "Two in a Row," "Four Quarters."

The goal is always the same: To give Curry a way to continue improving and to stave off the kind of complacency that could leave him stagnant. "No matter how great people tell you that you are or how lucky or inadequate critics say you are," advises Curry, it's important to "find that will to keep going."

STAT ⚡ Coming off their **NBA championship** in 2015, Curry and the Warriors were annoyed by the lack of respect given to their accomplishment, as many pundits declared it a fluke. They set out to show just how good they were the following season, and got off to a league-record 24-0 start. They then eclipsed the all-time record for wins in a season, with 73.

He knew that meeting challenges and raising the bar higher and higher was the only way to get better, so he never shied away from it.

"You have to go to find the best. That's going to elevate you. You can't live off the crumbs of the competition. You actually have to go find the best because that's going to sharpen your toolkit even more."

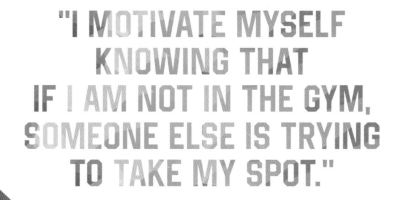

"I MOTIVATE MYSELF KNOWING THAT IF I AM NOT IN THE GYM, SOMEONE ELSE IS TRYING TO TAKE MY SPOT."

As Curry's career drums onward, even with four championships, two MVP trophies, and a 3-point shooting record highlighting his Hall-of-Fame resume, he has to keep feeding his fire. The NBA is too competitive to sit back on your accomplishments. One thing that fuels him is the certainty that if he gets complacent, he will lose his place as the best shooter in the NBA.

LIFE LESSONS FROM A LEGEND

- NO MATTER YOUR POSITION, YOU CAN ALWAYS LEAD BY EXAMPLE.
- HONOR YOUR COMMITMENTS FULLY.
- ALWAYS PUSH YOUR LIMITS.
- DON'T LET COMPLACENCY SLOW YOU DOWN.

LOOK BEYOND
YOURSELF

CHAPTER 5

One summer, Shonn Brown, who had coached Stephen Curry as a high-schooler at Charlotte Christian, was invited to help out at Curry's basketball camp in the city for a few days. Brown obliged. He had maintained contact with Curry over the years and was happy to help. When the camp was over, Brown approached Curry and thanked him for the opportunity.

It had seemed like a lifetime ago that Brown first got hold of Curry as a 14-year-old. Much had changed. Brown had remained a high school coach, and a good one. Curry, though, had turned himself into the game's greatest shooter, perhaps of all time. He could retire on the spot and still be a Naismith Basketball Hall of Fame player. In the hoops hierarchy, Curry was roundball royalty, and Brown was but a humble

"I REPRESENT GOD, I REPRESENT MY FAMILY, I REPRESENT THE PEOPLE THAT HAVE POURED INTO ME."

citizen. It was that dynamic that spurred Brown to thank Curry for letting him be there at his camp.

Curry raised an eyebrow. "You're Coach Brown," he finally said, puzzled. "You're my Coach Brown."

He looked at Brown much as he did when he was a teenager—as an authority figure with basketball wisdom, as someone who passed on that wisdom to others graciously. Brown was still a coach, his coach, and even with NBA stardom under his belt, Curry still felt like he worked for Brown (not the other way around). That's just Curry's way. He holds tight to and respects the coaches (among other people) who helped him along his way, who molded his individual brilliance into a team concept:

"[Coach Brown] saw me when I was fourteen, sixteen, eighteen years old, and those were some interesting years. He set the vision for what I could accomplish going forward in life, not just in basketball."

LANDSLIDE VICTORY

Curry made history when he became the only player to be named the unanimous MVP in 2015–16, receiving all 131 first-place votes. If you think that does not matter much to Curry, think again: He named the media company he founded "Unanimous."

One of Brown's challenges early in Curry's prep career was getting him to put up more shots. He had the sterling form he'd learned from his father, and was the team's best scorer, but Curry didn't want to take chances away from other players. Curry was too unselfish to focus on his own scoring.

Still, Brown pushed the issue. He told Curry: "Steph, we need you to score. We need you to shoot more."

"But what are the guys on the team going to think? I'm a point guard," Curry responded.

Brown came up with a compromise.

"Hey, four shots a quarter," Brown told him. "Sixteen a game. Because I think you're going to make at least half of them, if not more."

Brown was right. Curry, despite being careful about shooting too much, finished his career at Charlotte Christian as the school's all-time leading scorer, and the Knights went 33-3 in his senior season.

BE COACHABLE

One universally accepted truth about Steph Curry is that his unselfishness and team-first disposition is not an act—he is authentic in his desire to put winning above all, something that has been ingrained in him since he first started taking basketball seriously. Curry has a soft-spoken demeanor and would much rather be led by a strong coach than have to do the leading himself; he would rather be an active rook on the chessboard than a king.

"I KNEW I DID NOT KNOW IT ALL, I KNEW I HAD A LOT TO LEARN, AND A LOT OF ROOM TO GROW."

Curry was lucky, in his youth, to have coaches like Brown and Davidson's Bob McKillop, who has maintained a uniquely strong bond with Curry over the years, both being a major part of the other's legacy. Coaching young Curry required a delicate balance, simultaneously encouraging his talent while accommodating his desire to keep his teammates involved. He was never going to be particularly tall or athletic, which meant he was destined to be a point guard, and point guards had to pass the ball.

Curry made being coached relatively easy, though. One of the benefits of being as lightly recruited as Curry turned out to be is that

Curry never suffered from the delusion that he knew the game better than his coaches:

> *"I am thankful because I wanted it so bad that I was cool accepting being coached. . . . I was OK with getting coached, no matter how tough it was, no matter how embarrassing it was. I am thankful that I accepted that early so I could go through those lumps and not lose confidence."*

It's hard for him to understand why, even at the NBA level, players could pass up extra coaching. He works all offseason with his trainer, Brandon Payne, and leans on Warriors assistant coach Bruce Fraser during the year to help with his workouts and drills.

To turn down opportunities to work with teachers like those implies that a player has nothing in his game that needs improvement.

Only a perfect player has nothing to improve, and to Curry there are no perfect players. He knows that listening to an objective voice can give you more insight into improving any weaknesses. Curry craves the self-improvement that coaches bring:

> *"That's the only way you are going to get to your full potential, that is the only way you're going to get exposed to where you can look yourself in the mirror and say, 'This is what I need to work on, these are the strides I need to take to get to where I want to be.'"*

When Curry arrived at Golden State, his fellow Warriors did not have a reputation for diligence or work ethic. After the team's practices, the gym would routinely clear out, players scattering back to their homes. He wanted to change that, not by declaring it a new team policy or by bullying his teammates into extra work. Curry did it quietly, a slow-dripping faucet, by just showing up each day and doing the work. He would stay after practice and players who noticed his improvement began to join him. As he rose to become the team's best player, he maintained his habit, and it sent a powerful message to the rest of the team: If extra work is good enough for the star, it should be good enough for you.

"THAT'S WHAT I TELL EVERYONE: BE OPEN TO BEING COACHED."

As the Warriors started winning more, their practice facility turned into one of the liveliest spots in the NBA, with as much activity after practice as there had been during practice.

That's the power of Steph Curry. Without saying much, he made an entire team coachable.

"It's all a part of the process of, like, taking bits and pieces from different personalities and characters that you come across," Curry said, referring to the influence of coaches he's had along the way and what he's learned from them. As far as who contributed most to his success, his answer is simple: "They all have— ever since my college—my high school years, basically, everybody's had a piece of that."

BE A LEADER, YOUR WAY

In the 2012 offseason, when Curry still was recovering from his second round of ankle surgeries, general manager Bob Myers approached him with a request. "If you come out of this healthy," Myers asked, "can you work on leading this team?"

The question was problematic for Curry. He had been a leader in high school and college, but he led by example in those days. He was certain always to conduct himself as though he was just another player on the 12-man roster, no more or less important than anyone else. He did not know whether he could "work" on leadership. What did that mean? Get involved with play-calling? Yell and scream more? Read more books on leadership? He intended to stay

STAT ⚡ **No player, even one as great as Curry, can be an expert in everything. The slam dunk might be the most exciting play in basketball, but don't expect to see any from Curry. In his career, he has had just 26 dunks and stopped attempting them after he turned 30.**

"I HAD TO GROW INTO THE ROLE OF LEADERSHIP, AND IN MANY WAYS, I'M STILL GROWING INTO IT."

true to his personality and beliefs as a man and as a player, so he needed time to figure out what his style of leadership looked like:

> *"To realize the opportunity I had to not only be a great basketball player but to walk into a role of leadership, that wasn't going to be easy but demanded another level of awareness and commitment, consistency, and wisdom. I had to figure that out for myself."*

Curry also had to consider the locker room. When he was a young player, he leaned on Warriors veterans like Richard Jefferson and Jarrett Jack for experience and vocal leadership. As he matured, the Warriors brought on tirelessly vocal defensive star Draymond Green, the very eccentric Klay Thompson, and the forcefully intellectual and experienced Andre Iguodala. It was important to Curry to not try to be all things:

> *"We have different players in this locker room with different styles of leadership. We have just about every element covered between our vets, so it's easy for me to be myself and lead my way. I don't have to be demonstrative; we have someone like that. I've always been a lead-by-example person."*

Curry was not out to seize control of the team from any of those players. He wanted to set an example for teammates, and use his voice only when needed. What emerged was

"THAT'S THE COMMON THREAD WITH GREAT LEADERS. . . . THEY'RE ALWAYS LEARNING, THEY'RE ALWAYS CHALLENGING THEMSELVES, AND THEY THRIVE MOSTLY WHEN IT'S UNCOMFORTABLE."

"I KNOW HOW TO WORK HARD, AND I LIKE TO LET THAT SPEAK FOR ME."

Curry's unique style of leadership, one that emphasized supporting his entire team and taking on more accountability for what the team could do as a whole:

> *"You need [a leader] to pour a vision into you in terms of what you're capable of, what your full potential is, not just as a player but as someone who can impact the locker room in different ways, can impact the organization through leadership, through walking into accountability."*

BE INCLUSIVE

Curry revels in being a good teammate, in being an essential component of the Warriors' machine. He has, over the years, put together an extensive highlight reel, but the most satisfying plays tend to be those in which he sets up another player, either directly or indirectly. One of his favorite career moments came when his fellow star guard, Klay Thompson, rattled off 60 points in just three quarters. During the game, Curry can be seen celebrating wildly, as if he had been the one who scored all those points.

In 2018, when Curry was out for three weeks because of an ankle injury, the Warriors had to call on journeyman Quinn Cook to help fill his void. Golden State would need Cook to start at guard in Curry's place, the first time he had ever been an NBA starter. He was nervous.

"I THINK YOUR TEAMMATES RESPECT YOU WHEN YOU'RE BEING TRUE TO YOURSELF."

Curry stepped in to make the transition smooth, calling Cook and arranging a meeting an hour before the game. He laid out what Cook could expect to see on the floor during the game, and, at halftime, he met with him again.

Cook struggled at first as a starter, but with Curry's backing, gained confidence and scored 25 points in his fourth game in the role. He scored 28 in his fifth game, two of the best performances of his career. That is a key difference for the Warriors compared with many other teams: Players care about each other, and the last guy on the bench gets brought along in much the same way as the star. Every individual has value:

"We feel like something good is going to happen, if everybody on the team or everybody on the court touches the ball and feels involved. Whether it's me shooting or (not) at the end of the possession, if everybody touches it and has an opportunity to feel involved in that play, then something good is going to happen."

Often, Curry creates opportunities for other players just by being on the floor. He is the point guard, but he frequently gives the ball up quickly because defenses give him extra attention. Curry likes to wend his way around the court, pulling opponents toward him so that a teammate can spring free for a wide-open shot:

"I love the style of being able to play on and off the ball, just the chaos that you can create, even if I don't have [the ball]. Those possessions are mad fun to me because you get off the ball, you run down the lane, you come off a screen, two people come with you, and somebody gets a layup. That brings joy to the way I approach the game."

SHARE THE JOURNEY

One of the behind-the-scenes features of the Warriors since Curry joined has been their togetherness, and their appreciation of all the team staff who help make them successful, from Curry and head coach Steve Kerr down to the least-used player on the team's bench, the video coordinator, and the equipment manager. When the team is at home and has a break, Curry—and other players—often host parties and organize dinners for the team and staff.

"EVERYBODY'S GOING TO LOOK GOOD IF EVERYBODY'S INVOLVED."

"IN OUR LOCKER ROOM, IT'S AN OPEN SPACE WHERE THERE'S NO JUDGMENT."

On the road, the team books space in a restaurant for all the players and traveling staff to gather and interact. The team picks up the bill:

"We want to be able to include everybody in that process . . . so we can all get to know each other and understand when we come to work, everybody has a different story that they're bringing with them, and it's an important story."

Around the NBA, that level of unity is seldom seen.

"We play opposing teams, and they come in, hear about these dinners, hear about certain things that we do as a team, and they look at us like, 'Are you all serious?' Like, 'We don't get that,'" Curry said.

The Warriors also pride themselves on having a peaceful locker-room culture, where all players have equal say. That is not to say there are no issues between players, that arguments and tension never test the team's unity. But there is an atmosphere of acceptance.

"Whether you're mad at somebody for not setting a screen, or your kids kept you up all night, or whatever the case may be, we have the environment, we have the settings where you're able to bring whatever is on your mind to the table, and everybody values that."

That is part of the culture that Curry helped to establish, so that the Warriors seek out players and coaches who fit that mold. They might pass on adding someone with talent if the front office does not think the player would mesh, chemistry-wise, with the rest of the team.

PUT THE GROUP OVER THE INDIVIDUAL

A funny thing happened as the Warriors' culture changed: The team started to put winning ahead of everything else.

First, the Warriors earned a 47-35 record and a playoff spot in 2013, followed by 51 wins and another playoff appearance in 2014. Prior to the 2014–15 season, the Warriors added head coach Steve Kerr, who had been a role player on five championship teams during his playing career. In Kerr's first season as coach, the Warriors won 67 games and

"IT'S NOT ABOUT ME."

"IT'S NOT ABOUT INDIVIDUAL AWARDS. IT'S NOT ABOUT ALL-STAR APPEARANCES. IT'S ABOUT WINNING A CHAMPIONSHIP AND DOING ANYTHING YOU CAN TO GET TO THAT LEVEL."

were crowned NBA champs after defeating LeBron James and the Cleveland Cavaliers.

The Warriors were rebuilt with talent, character, and the occasional bit of humor, necessities for NBA teams hoping to grind through an 82-game season, and another 20-25 postseason games.

Team unity and good chemistry doesn't come out of nowhere. According to Curry, what it takes is "everybody committing 100% to whatever that role is that you're asked to do—being selfless and being able to sacrifice in that role, and understanding that we're all going to get the glory and the praise when we go through our experiences."

Change at the top was helpful. The team got a new ownership group dedicated to professionalism and the pursuit of winning, as well as a new, championship-caliber coach. Curry called it "the perfect storm."

For decades, the Warriors had been a fun team to watch—fast-paced, packed with offbeat characters. They were the NBA's loveable losers. Curry was not going to stand for that, and as new threads to the Warriors' story emerged—a new coach, a new general

A WARM WELCOME

In the summer of 2016, after the Warriors had been upset by the Cavaliers in the NBA Finals, the team had enough cap room to do something audacious: Sign Oklahoma City Thunder superstar Kevin Durant in free agency. Durant was interested, but he had one big concern: He was afraid that Curry wouldn't be okay with him joining. Few NBA stars want to share the court with another star player. Curry put Durant's anxiety to rest with a long text message that ended with, "It does not matter whether you are MVP or I am MVP. If it is you, I will be sitting there in the front row to congratulate you."

"I'VE ALWAYS BELIEVED THAT SUCCESS FOR ANYONE IS ALL ABOUT DRIVE, DEDICATION, AND DESIRE, BUT FOR ME, IT'S ALSO BEEN ABOUT CONFIDENCE AND FAITH."

"I KNOW WHEN TO
GET OUT THE WAY,
I KNOW WHEN
TO LEAD,
I KNOW WHEN
TO SPEAK,
I KNOW HOW TO FIND
VALUE IN MYSELF
EVERY SINGLE DAY."

manager, new ownership, new players—his desire to drop the losing image became clear:

"Forget about days of the past even though it was an exciting brand of basketball. It wasn't anything that was championship driven. Those different storylines all merged into one theme at the right time, and we never looked back."

LIFE LESSONS FROM A LEGEND

- **REMEMBER THOSE WHO HELPED YOU ON YOUR WAY UP.**
- **LOOK FOR LESSONS OTHERS CAN TEACH YOU.**
- **CREATE UNITY AMONG THOSE AROUND YOU.**
- **DON'T FORCE LEADERSHIP; LEAD IN YOUR OWN STYLE.**

PRACTICE IRRATIONAL CONFIDENCE

When Steph Curry was a high school freshman, he was given a choice: He could take a high-usage spot on the junior varsity team, where he would be a starter and the team leader, or he could push himself to level up and earn a place with the varsity. Playing varsity might mean sitting on the bench more than being on the floor, but it would put Curry with his school's best players. Maybe he could work his way into becoming a necessary part of the team's rotation.

But maybe not. Curry was afraid of getting lost on the bench, and played it safe. He took the playing time and the spot on the JV:

"I think I took the easy way out trying to play JV and never really putting myself out there and shooting for the moon. And about halfway through my JV

season, I was starting to regret it because I really felt like I was good enough to play at the next level, but I didn't really have the belief to put that into action."

Curry vowed that he would not let that nervousness make decisions for him in the future.

Curry, from then on, would shoot for the moon. It was around this time, perhaps, that Curry's irrational confidence was born.

ESTABLISH A HIGH STANDARD

Early on in his career at Davidson, Curry had an epiphany. He had grown up watching Indiana Pacers star Reggie Miller, the greatest shooter of his era. Because Curry was a pretty good shooter himself— and with good bloodlines for the job—he looked at Miller as a player to emulate as his career moved forward. But he had also become fascinated with the breakneck pace and creativity of Phoenix Suns point guard Steve Nash, who was, like Curry, undersized and not

"I TOLD MYSELF I WOULD NEVER BE TIMID ABOUT ANYTHING LIKE THAT EVER AGAIN."

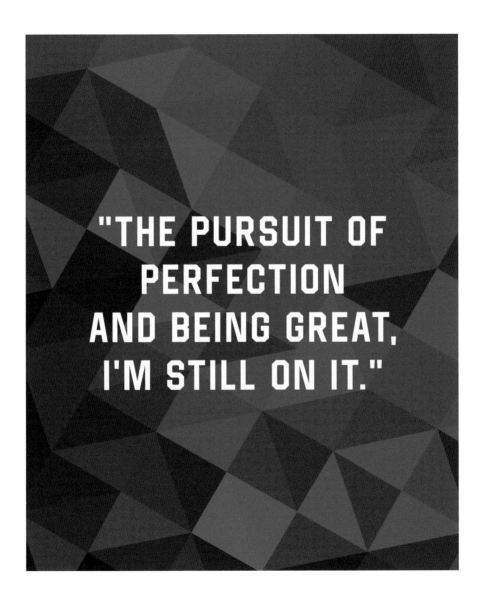

"THE PURSUIT OF PERFECTION AND BEING GREAT, I'M STILL ON IT."

particularly athletic. Curry could imagine himself modeling his game after Nash, too:

> *"Watching Nash be a pick-and-roll master, all the different passes he would make, his tight handle, and he was not the most athletic guy, and that resonated with me. Reggie played against my dad, so every time he played against him, if Reggie was on the court, I just watched everything he did—the angles he took, the deception, the wild push-offs he would have. All that stuff, I was a fan of it."*

Inspiration struck. Why not pattern his game after *both?*

"When I understood my skill set," Curry later explained, "it was clear that I could mesh those two guys as a baseline of how I wanted to play, and then take it from there, hanging [my] hat on that style of play."

This was a goal that some might have thought was beyond Curry's reach. At the time, Nash was a two-time MVP bound for the Hall of Fame, while Miller was already in the Hall of Fame and had retired as the NBA's all-time most prolific 3-point shooter. Here was Curry, a young guard toiling for a mid-major college in the Sun Belt Conference, making plans to take the best aspects of both stars, combine them into his wispy body, and take the NBA by storm.

STAT ⚡ For the first time in his four NBA Finals appearances, Curry was named the series MVP in the Warriors' win over the Boston Celtics in 2022 (he lost out to Andre Iguodala in 2015 and Kevin Durant in 2017 and 2018). Curry was brilliant in the Celtics series, averaging 31.2 points, 6 rebounds, and 5 assists, making 43.7% of his 3-pointers.

"THINK ABOUT SETTING
HIGH EXPECTATIONS,
A HIGH BAR
FOR YOURSELF,
SO YOU CAN GET
BETTER AND BETTER
AND BETTER."

Some might have laughed. Others might have found it absurd to think he could reach that level. This was the same Curry, after all, who two years earlier had been unable to drum up interest from a single major-conference college. But Curry had long before made a decision not to limit himself, not to let preconceived notions of what was possible define his dreams. Curry knew what he could do, even if few others did.

Besides, he had one of his biggest confidence boosters by his side nearly every day—Bob McKillop, the Davidson coach. McKillop was one of the few to see past Curry's lack of size and recognize his brilliance as a shooter. Although he was a point guard in high school, Curry played more shooting guard for the Wildcats, a role that McKillop encouraged since it allowed him to be more creative with his game. Because Curry put in the work (and then some), McKillop never so much as raised an eyebrow when Curry took an unwise shot, and did not sweat his star's occasional struggles:

"He told me when I was a freshman that I had license to shoot any shot I wanted, but I'd have to work for it. I'd have to put in the time and actually commit to learning on the job. Even when I failed early freshman year, he stayed in my ear because he saw my potential before I did."

Curry likely would not have enjoyed the kind of freedom he had at Davidson if he'd signed on with a bigger program. The space his coach gave him to experiment with his game allowed Curry's creativity to run loose. Unlike a lot of college players, he knew that if he tried something and it did not work, he wouldn't be relegated to the bench.

He developed new ways of getting open looks coming off screens or on curls, worked on his stop-and-start game, birthed a delicate floater in the lane, and discovered that an open look, even from well behind the 3-point line, was still a good shot, as long as he was the one shooting it.

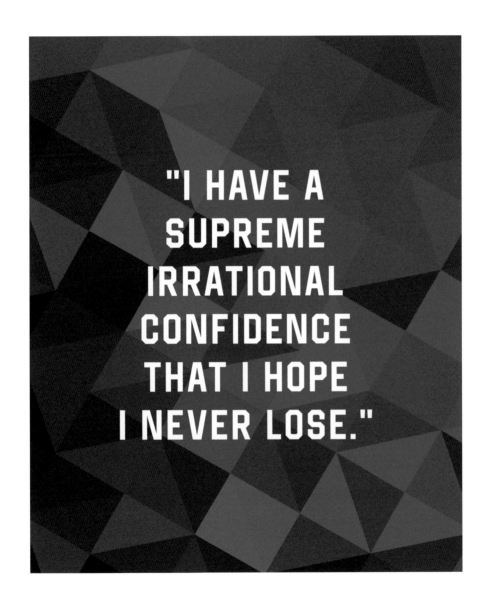

"I HAVE A SUPREME IRRATIONAL CONFIDENCE THAT I HOPE I NEVER LOSE."

"I FEEL LIKE
I CAN DO ANYTHING."

Curry had the irrational confidence required to transform from a college player into an NBA phenom.

TRY SOMETHING NEW

Curry and the Warriors made their first playoff appearance against Denver in 2013, and in Game 4 of that series (the Warriors had won two of the first three games), the Warriors took a 12-point lead at halftime in a most unusual way—two big guys, Andrew Bogut and Carl Landry, scored 12 points each. Curry made one shot from the field in the half, and scored just 7 points.

But that quickly changed, as Curry found the hot hand in the third quarter. He tried 11 shots and made 8 of them in the period, tallying 22 points. He also tried something new with 23 seconds to go in the period: He attempted a 3-pointer in the left corner just in front of the Nuggets' bench, with the Denver players, primarily center JaVale McGee, shouting at him to distract him.

As Curry shot, he held up one hand and turned toward McGee, his back now to the basket. He smiled and began running back up the court, while the ball was in the air. This was new. Was he trying a *no-look 3-pointer*? Yep. If Curry had not been sure that the shot went in, the sold-out crowd at Oracle Arena let him know when it erupted in cheers.

It's hard to say where that moment originated, but Curry tried to explain it:

> *"For some reason, I just got an out-of-body experience. I shot it. Literally, as I let it go, I was like, 'I've never felt a shot feel better than that.' I turned around and kind of looked at JaVale and then just ran off, and it went in."*

Curry liked the cockiness of the sequence, the way it deflated the Nuggets (who were outscored by the Warriors by 25 points in the quarter thereafter), and from then on, the no-look 3-pointer became one of the shots he would pull out on an opponent when he was in a good rhythm.

He made the shot twice in the 2022 NBA All-Star Game. He's put two of them on the Timberwolves, two on the Trail Blazers, and has made no-look threes against the Lakers, Bulls, and Spurs. He even shot one in Game 3 of the Western Conference Finals in 2022, turning to look, tongue extended, at the Mavericks' bench. That irritated Mavs star Luka Doncic, and the pair had a brief altercation during the subsequent time-out.

It was not something Curry had worked on in practice, not something he had tested in some listless preseason game. He broke it out in the most important game of his career to that point:

> *"It was kind of a really special moment. Just, I don't know, the irrational confidence to even try it in a playoff game. But it was dope."*

It remains a bad idea to antagonize Curry on a basketball court, especially when he is starting a hot streak.

BE BOLD

When Curry takes the floor for an NBA game, his shyness falls away and he becomes more of a performer than he is in his day-

"THE ONE-HANDERS, THE TURNOVERS, THE SHOTS I TAKE AND THE WAY I PLAY, YOU CAN GET LOST IN IT, THAT IS THE CONFIDENCE I HAVE."

to-day life. While you wouldn't loop him in with the league's big-time trash-talkers, he does play with a certain amount of swagger, and incorporates a touch of showmanship to punctuate his successes. For much of his career, though, Curry's go-to taunt has been the shimmy.

In one game against Portland in the second round of the 2016 playoffs, soon after Curry had returned from an injury, his shot was off. He missed his first 10 3-point tries, and did not make one until there were just under five minutes to play in the fourth quarter. When the shot sank, Curry went into a full-body shimmy.

Warriors coach Steve Kerr turned to one of his assistant coaches and said, "Is he shimmying? He's 1-for-11 from three. You better believe in yourself when you're shimmying at 1-for-11."

Curry has no shortage of belief in himself, even when he is 0-for-10. His on-court antics, whether it's a no-look three or a shoulder shimmy, serve a purpose—they fire

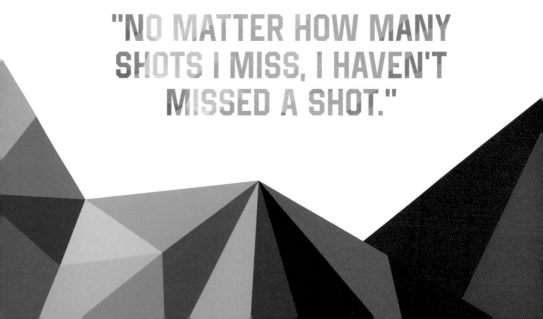

"NO MATTER HOW MANY SHOTS I MISS, I HAVEN'T MISSED A SHOT."

MOVES LIKE CURRY

If you want to see what Curry's confidence looks like, here are three of his key moves:

- **THE SHIMMY.** This is Curry's most frequently used taunt, often coming after a 3-pointer at a key moment. It's been used against Curry at times by rival stars like Luka Doncic and Chris Paul.

- **THE NO-LOOK 3-POINTER.** Bad enough when a team leaves Curry alone to knock down a 3-pointer. Worse when he turns to look at them before the ball even goes into the basket. Curry estimates he makes about 80% of them. The ones he misses are embarrassing but, he said, "I just run back hard on defense and pretend it didn't happen."

- **NIGHT-NIGHT.** Here, Curry puts his hands together and rests his cheek on them, as if going to sleep. The move originated during the 2022 playoffs in a win over Denver, and Curry explained it emerged from repeatedly telling himself, "Put 'em to sleep. Put 'em to sleep."

up his confidence and remind him how great he can be. That was true in the game against the Blazers, when he bounced back from a slow start and wound up developing a hot hand for the rest of the game, even into overtime. Curry set an NBA record for points in an overtime period, scoring 17. He was not all that concerned about the 10 misses.

Around the Curry family, the uber-confident alter ego that flashes itself at game time is known as "Wardell." That's Curry's given name—Wardell Stephen Curry II. Wardell was his father Dell's full name, but it was also his grandfather's name. When Curry allows himself to get a little cocky, like when he celebrates the vanquishing of an

"I CREATE MY OWN REALITY."

opponent, he is channeling the family's history of competitiveness. It's a welcome feeling:

"You're invincible. Everybody says it is the Wardell in me, the family bloodline. I don't know, but it is a supreme confidence that's based on the work you put in. But it is an irrational confidence. It is one of the best feelings in the world, when it comes on the court, how you express yourself."

Not everyone appreciates the Wardell show—Doncic is one of a long list of players annoyed by Curry's dances. But that doesn't really bother him: "It's amazing, because it is authentic, in terms of me just enjoying myself out

---

STAT ⚡ **Fifty-four is a pretty big number when it comes to Steph Curry's legacy. That was his point total in a game at Madison Square Garden in New York on February 27, 2013, a game widely considered Curry's NBA breakout performance, televised on ESPN. Curry made 11 of his 13 3-point attempts in the game.**

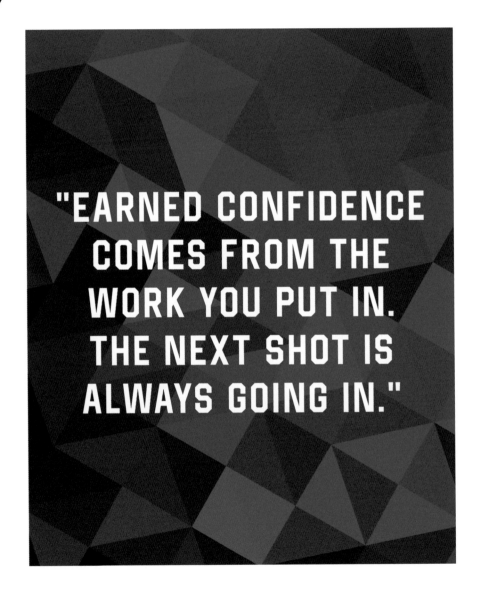

"EARNED CONFIDENCE COMES FROM THE WORK YOU PUT IN. THE NEXT SHOT IS ALWAYS GOING IN."

there," Curry says, explaining why he can't help but keep doing the shimmy. The negative reactions from some players carry little weight: "I get that it is going to be, 'This (jerk) right here . . .' a lot of the time."

The delusional state of mind that allows Curry to erase his misses, forget his failures, invent new shots, and shoot for the moon is a crucial component in his incredible success:

"I'll take shots from all over the court no matter (what). Everybody'll look at me like, 'Why did you shoot that?' I really have full confidence in what I'm doing now based off the past. . . . So that's my delusion for sure."

USE YOUR INSECURITIES

Of course, Curry would not be human if he walked in pure assurance, if there was no measure of self-doubt. But when he does scrutinize himself, he sees his failings as only temporary, things he can fix with time and

"IT'S WAY HARDER TO STAY AT THIS LEVEL THAN TO GET HERE."

"I NEVER WORRY ABOUT MY SHOT, EVER."

effort. Even at his peak, Curry never accepted that he had reached his potential, or that there was nothing new he could add to his game.

He pointed to the 2022 NBA Finals, in which Golden State defeated the Boston Celtics, and Curry won the series MVP trophy. He was proud of his team, and proud of his individual accomplishment, but he found himself unable to sleep three nights later, worrying about whether he could follow up on that success. "It is almost like the impostor syndrome," he explains.

He has two inner voices, a sort of devil of doubt on one side and an angel of confidence on the other. One sounds like comedian Kevin Hart, shrill and dismissive, saying things like:

"'Man, you ain't nothing. Ah, man, you're not gonna do nothing.' Just ragging on you the whole time. It probably would-be Kobe's voice on the other side, like that killer instinct, that you're ready for pretty much any situation, knowing who you are."

One voice tells him he can make any shot and the other says he'll never make it. The way Curry bridges the gap between his confidence and his insecurity is through hard work. Doing the work gives Curry some comfort, reassures him that he can keep breaking new ground, keep innovating. It's work that eases his healthy insecurity and transforms his irrational confidence into what Curry calls "earned confidence":

"There's a confidence . . . that I have the ability and the skill set to win any game, any night. That's something that's only built on the shoulders of the work you put in. Not to be clichéd, but that's really how I gain that confidence and maintain that from year after year."

By the time he shoots the ball, he is already benefitting from that self-assurance.

LIFE LESSONS FROM A LEGEND

- DON'T SHORTCHANGE YOURSELF OR THE POSSIBILITIES AHEAD OF YOU.

- EXCEED THE LIMITS AND PUSH THE BOUNDARIES OF YOUR ROLE.

- BACK UP BOLD IDEAS AND TEMPER INSECURITY WITH HARD WORK.

"EVERY TIME
I RISE UP,
I HAVE CONFIDENCE
THAT I'M GOING
TO MAKE IT."

CHANGE THE GAME

The tale of the 3-pointer's development and importance in the history of the NBA—and in all of basketball, really—can be best told through simple numbers attached to two players known for their proclivity for those deep shots: Dell Curry and his oldest child, Steph Curry. When Dell Curry entered the NBA out of Virginia Tech in 1986, the average NBA team took 4.7 3-point tries per game. They made 30.1% of them. By the time Dell retired in 2002, the average NBA team was shooting 14.7 threes per game and making 35.4% of those attempts.

Seven years later, in 2009, Steph Curry came into the NBA after leaving Davidson, and the league had seen a rise in 3-point shots between his father's final game and Steph's NBA debut. The average team was taking 18.1 threes per game, and making 35.5% of them.

Move ahead just 12 years, to 2021, the season in which Curry set the all-time record for made 3-pointers, breaking Ray Allen's record. That year, the average team in the league took 35.2 3-pointers per game, nearly double the number of threes attempted in Curry's rookie year. In just two generations of Currys in the NBA, the 3-pointer grew by almost 750%.

Curry accepts the assertion that he is the primary driver of that explosion, arguably the most significant change in the NBA since the advent of the shot clock in the league's early days. There were other factors—the growth of advanced statistics, rule changes, teams that dedicated themselves to playing with a faster tempo—but Curry is the player who pushed all those factors to their most extreme conclusion:

"I fully acknowledge that I've changed the way basketball is played and approached, not just on our level, but all the way down to the grassroots level. For better or for worse."

Go back to his father's rookie year, and you'll find that the Mavericks led the NBA in 3-point shots made as a team, with 231. Steph Curry surpassed that number, by himself, five years in a row, leading the NBA in 3-pointers each season.

FIND YOUR EDGE

In the beginning, Curry's status as a change agent was a matter of necessity. He did not arrive in the NBA the way other stars did—like LeBron James, the forward with the body of a linebacker, or Kevin Durant, who at more than 7 feet, was nearly a foot taller than Curry. Those players can boast talent, like Curry, and a maniacal work ethic, like Curry, but unlike Curry, they were also winners of a genetic lottery. Take LeBron, for example. At the draft combine in 2003, when LeBron was just 18, he was 6-foot-7 and weighed 245 pounds.

"MAKE IT WORK NO MATTER WHAT YOU HAVE TO WORK WITH."

Curry needed to come up with unique ways to get to the basket and finish at the rim while protecting the ball, more of a challenge for a player of his height. He had to improve his ballhandling to the extent that it was flawless. Then he needed to take the moves he was coming up with and make them part of his muscle memory.

It was a familiar challenge to him, one that stretched all the way back to his childhood, back to the rickety hoop at his grandfather's house where his father had broken down his shot and rebuilt it over the course of a tear-soaked summer. The uneven, potholed ground in front of that hoop had forced him to find unusual ways to get the ball through the rim:

"[You have to] adjust. Get creative. Try a different angle, a different lane, a different move or a different shot—just make it work. Out there on my grandpa's court, there was no better place in the world to breed that kind of creativity."

Once he got past the ankle injuries in 2011 and 2012, Curry was determined to get back to his true self on the court, to be the kind of free-flowing player he had been in college, where Bob McKillop had told him he had the green light on any shot.

The Warriors had not given him that kind of freedom since he came on board in 2009. They

MAKE YOUR MENTORS PROUD

Curry found himself in the company of two players he idolized: Reggie Miller and Ray Allen. Miller held the 3-point record (with 2,560 3-pointers made) until 2011, when it was broken by Allen, who retired with 2,973 3-pointers on his resume. A decade after that, Curry was able to top Allen and become the league's all-time 3-point king. He accepted the award at Madison Square Garden with both Allen and Miller in attendance.

were trying to figure out in which box he belonged—was he a point guard or a shooter? Was he Steve Nash or Reggie Miller? Curry got back to his roots and remembered that he had set out to be both, a daring ballhandler and a deadeye deep shooter, even if there was no precedent for his style in the NBA:

> *"It was really honing in and adapting a style that wasn't really accepted before in terms of the way that I approach the game from a creativity, shot-selection, creativity, and joy perspective."*

BE INNOVATIVE

On the basketball floor, Curry is an artist in his own right. "I, obviously, have a natural eye for the rim,"

he said, "and feel and touch and creativity and all that. And I can see angles. So that's the art."

Artists, poets, musicians—anyone who produces creative work has a point of inspiration that leads them to conceive of something truly new and groundbreaking. Curry's art begins with a need. Innovation is a necessity in pro basketball if you want to outperform the competition. The NBA has a limited population and unlimited technology— everyone knows what everyone else is doing. If Curry adds an element to his game, like a new dribble move, or a new way of getting open for a shot, that move has a shelf life. Eventually, scouts and coaches will identify what he is doing, defenders

"FOUR IDEALS THAT DESCRIBE THE JOURNEY THE BEST WAY I KNOW HOW: THAT IS FAITH, PASSION, DRIVE, AND WILL."

"AROUND YEAR 2 IN THE LEAGUE, THAT WAS WHEN I REALLY UNDERSTOOD BEING CREATIVE ABOUT HOW I CAN PLAY."

will study him closely on film, and the power of his innovation will dissipate as soon as other players learn to anticipate the move.

So, Curry will, as he says, "go back to the lab" to think of something else to try, work on it with his trainer or coaches, repeat it until it becomes part of his muscle memory, then break it out during a game.

Curry gets a thrill when it works, when he can take the germ of an idea for a move from his imagination and

bring it to the practice court, then into game situations. After his first year with the Warriors, he began leaning in to his power to innovate:

"Visualizing stuff that maybe I haven't done before, and then trying it in a skill session or a practice or whatnot. That confidence that comes behind that is intoxicating. And then you get in the game and you lose yourself in that. Then you go back to the drawing board and keep doing that over and over and over again."

"YOU DON'T WANT TO FALL INTO THE TRAP OF COMPARING YOURSELF TO OTHER GREAT SHOOTERS. WHAT YOU WANT TO COMPARE YOURSELF TO IS YOU."

"ONCE YOU HIT A COUPLE AND IT'S NOT LUCK, YOU ESTABLISH, 'THIS IS WHERE I'M AT.'"

TAKE THE LONG SHOT

The explosion of the 3-pointer is the most obvious way Curry has affected the NBA, but it goes beyond the quantity of threes he attempts. It's also the location of those threes. The 3-point line is 22 feet from the basket at its shortest distance, and 23.9 feet at its longest distance. Logic dictates that the closer a player is to the basket, the more accurate the shot will be, and thus, players traditionally do their best to get as close to the line as possible.

But teams are generally adept at guarding shooters at the 3-point line. Curry figured they were a lot less adept if he launched a shot a few feet behind the line—say, 28, 30 feet. The added distance made for a less accurate shot, but Curry felt that taking shots from those spots, without a defender around him, more than counterbalanced the loss of accuracy.

For him, at least. Curry is quick to point out that pushing the game increasingly past the 3-point line is not for everyone. It requires some effort:

"I did not have that range the first couple [of] years in the league. It became a reaction to the way the defense was guarding me—where is the most amount of space?... It's a good feeling to have because you know you can surprise defenses with it."

STAY AHEAD OF THE GAME

As Curry's NBA success grew, with an MVP award in 2015 followed by the only unanimous MVP award in league history in 2016, plus championships in 2015, 2017, 2018, and 2022, it was impossible for the rest of the league not to take notice. Other star players followed suit, plucking the moves they liked from Curry's repertoire.

That included the jump in 3-point tries. James Harden, also a member of the 2009 draft class, averaged just 3.9 3-point attempts in his first three seasons, but after Curry and the Warriors won the 2015 championship, he began chucking a lot more perimeter shots, eclipsing 8 for the first time the following year and spiking to 13.2 per game three years later. All-Stars like Damian Lillard and Paul George, too, pushed their 3-point numbers up.

Even the league's power forwards and centers, who traditionally stay around the basket, began working on their 3-point range. One of the most extreme examples was center Brook Lopez, a talented 7-footer who

"EVERYBODY'S GOT SPACE AT TWENTY-EIGHT FEET, BUT IS THAT A GOOD SHOT? PROBABLY NOT."

> ## "THE ABILITY TO CHANGE THE WAY PEOPLE APPROACH THE GAME IS UNREAL."

played mostly near the basket and made just three 3-point shots in the first eight seasons of his career. In the 2016–17 season, he made 134 3-pointers, and over the next four seasons, tallied more than 100 3-pointers each year.

The Warriors were well ahead of the rest of the league, though. For them, having so much good shooting meant that the floor was more spread, which reduced their need for big, lumbering players in the middle. The Warriors frequently went to a "small ball" style, in which their tallest player was 6-foot-8. The lineup was so effective it gained the nickname "the death lineup."

Sure enough, teams around the league emulated what the Warriors were doing. Curry was the fulcrum for all those changes within the team, and the catalyst for change around the NBA. He did it one step at a time, but he hadn't set out to transform the game. It was just a byproduct of his own creative process on the road, to being the best player he could be:

"I play the game the way I play, stretch the envelope, have a different level of creativity. I started shooting from deeper, build my range out. You add the ballhandling and the space creation to it."

Early in his NBA career, Curry was too focused on his own to-do list to notice how he was making an impact on how opponents constructed their rosters, and to reflect on how other star players (undersized guards especially) were borrowing from his repertoire. He would be asked about changing the sport, and he would scoff. But at this point in his career, it's evident even to him:

"You start to see teams be designed differently. You see guys that never prioritized 3-point shooting go to the lab in the summer and try to add it to their game. Everybody is opening their minds to what that can look like for them. What you see from me inspires you to add some form of it to your game, or open up the possibility of: 'Oh, hey, I can do that, too.'"

He's undoubtedly proud of the impact he's made, but he doesn't want to be satisfied with his contribution thus far. He doesn't want that sense of satisfaction to stifle his ambition while he is still an active player: "I am a little more reflective on that," he said. "I never let it get *too* far because I am still in it. I still feel like there is another level to get to."

OWN THE RIPPLE EFFECT

It takes innovation and dedication, in addition to talent, to create the kind of change in a profession that Curry brought to the NBA. Because everyone can shoot, even if they don't do it all that well, Curry's influence has exposed one of the key areas where all players can develop.

A player needs a certain amount of athleticism to dunk a basketball, a certain amount of agility to dribble effectively, and a certain amount of height to block a shot. But with

PGA FANTASIES

Curry has another obsession besides basketball: golf. He has a handicap that hovers between zero (a scratch golfer) and one, which puts him in the realm of the PGA. He calls golf "the little stepbrother" compared to basketball, but has wondered what might have been. "There was always that question," Curry said. "If I had put as much time into golf as I did basketball, could I have made it? We'll never know, but it's always competed in terms of my attention."

enough practice, anyone can get better at hurling a ball at the rim. Or as Curry puts it:

"Not everybody can just go and do calf raises and get a forty-inch vertical. Not everyone can just grow six inches and be taller. But you can shoot the ball. No matter what level you play, what league it is, it doesn't matter."

THE CURRY GENERATION

Curry is very popular among kids, and watching him play has inspired children and aspiring athletes in what's known as the "Curry Generation" to start hoisting shots from 25 feet away, no matter whether they've worked on those shots before. Curry has a sense of humor about it. He can't help but crack a smile as he explains the trend he started:

"Now you've got little kids and high school kids, middle school and younger, just jacking up threes, and parents and coaches get mad at me. . . . I did not say, 'Shoot that shot!'"

There are lessons that can be gleaned from Curry's audacious style of play, from his willingness to generate original ideas and his ability to put those ambitious ideas into action. That end product, the incredible play that leads to a score for Golden State, is the part we all see on television. Those stellar plays, he hopes, will inspire young people. At the same time, Curry wants to make sure they understand there's more to it than that miracle moment. There's a lot of sweat that goes into each of those plays. The message he'd give them is to slow down and take it step by step: "I am trying to level with them and say, there is a process to this."

LIFE LESSONS FROM A LEGEND

- DON'T LET PRECONCEIVED NOTIONS AFFECT HOW YOU SEE YOUR GOALS.
- BE ADAPTABLE; RECOGNIZE OPPORTUNITIES TO MAKE CHANGE.
- DEVELOP A MEANS FOR TURNING IDEAS INTO REALITY.

"HOPEFULLY, [MY CAREER] IS INSPIRATIONAL, SOMETHING THAT WILL LIVE FOREVER— HOW KIDS APPROACH THE GAME AND WHAT THEY CAN IMAGINE THEMSELVES DOING."

NEVER STOP GIVING BACK

In 2018, Steph Curry received a letter from nine-year-old Riley Morrison in Napa, California. She was writing to register a complaint of sorts. She was starting a new basketball season and was hoping to get a pair of Curry's new shoes from Under Armour, known as the Curry 5s. She and her father were "disappointed to see that there were no Curry 5s for sale under the girls section. However, they did have them for sale under the boys, even to customize," she wrote.

She went on to point out that Curry, with two daughters, has been supportive of girls in sports. But what about his shoes? "Girls want to rock the Curry 5s, too," she told him.

Curry did something few NBA superstars would do. He got a pen and paper and wrote back to Riley, telling her that he had spent the past two days talking to Under Armour about the issue and that, "We are fixing this NOW!!" He would send her a pair of the Curry 5s, and promised she would be the first kid to get the Curry 6s when they came out. He also extended an invitation to hang out with him on International Women's Day that March.

As far as customer service goes, Curry gets a five-star rating.

It is that sort of thing that has made Curry such an overwhelmingly popular star athlete. Because of his history as a skinny underdog in a big man's sport, he is easy to root for on the court, but because he does not treat others from the vantage point of the dispassionate star, because

he has maintained a normal-guy approach to his abnormal life, he is easy to root for off the court, too.

It is no act. It's not a series of publicity ploys. Curry has worked diligently off the court to have an impact, especially on kids throughout the Bay Area, and particularly in Oakland (where the Warriors played at Oracle Arena until 2019).

Curry has rebuilt courts throughout the city, refurbished school libraries, and visited food banks and women's shelters. He doesn't just write checks; he puts his feet where his money is. Curry shows up. NBA star Damian Lillard, an Oakland native, will vouch for that:

"WE LIVE IN A NICE LITTLE BUBBLE OF PLAYING BASKETBALL, BUT THERE ARE SOME REAL-WORLD ISSUES THAT ARE GOING ON."

"He did it right just by being himself. Anytime you are genuine and authentic, and then people get to witness your greatness like they've witnessed with Steph, it's easy to cheer for. You know you not supporting a facade or somebody that's pretending."

FOCUS YOUR PASSION

There is a reason why Curry is so dedicated to the city of Oakland, even now that the Warriors are in San Francisco: He was once a very happy resident. When most Warriors players were settling with their families in the wealthier suburbs of Oakland, Curry moved with his wife, Ayesha, right into Oakland's historic Jack London Square. He spent his first three years as a Warrior there:

"We understood, one, just the passion around the Warriors and sports. But also, just the passion for this area and what's come out of the city, how people from Oakland, when you ask them where they're from, they tell you, and there's a different tone that comes out of the pride of what the area means. And I think that struck me from day one."

As Curry's stature has grown, he and Ayesha formalized their charity work, setting up a foundation called "Eat. Learn. Play." to serve what the Currys feel is Oakland's most important population: kids. The foundation opened just before the onset of the COVID-19 pandemic. The Currys responded to a severe food crisis in the city by having 20 million meals delivered, mostly to children. They've also supported teacher-led literacy programs in the city and delivered more than 300,000 books to families. Living in Oakland gave him a perspective he could not have had otherwise.

Curry has also done charity work back at his home in Charlotte, and started a program in which he donates nets treated with insecticide to families in Africa to help stop the spread of malaria. After the 2012–13 season, Curry went to Africa to deliver the nets personally. It was the kind of trip that he could not have imagined taking as part of his NBA journey.

"There are a lot of different opportunities that basketball brings, and if you handle them the right way, a lot of good can come out of it: Obviously, the impact to the community, inspiring the next generation with whatever story you want to tell, and basically trying different opportunities and experiences that I never really thought possible without this game."

"GROWING UP, I SAW WHAT IT WAS LIKE TO BE A TRUE PROFESSIONAL IN THE SPOTLIGHT."

"I WANT TO CONTINUE TO HAVE A LEVEL OF IMPACT EVEN WHEN THE BALL STOPS BOUNCING."

BE GOOD TO KIDS

Spend a little time around the Warriors, and you are certain to see the team attracting a crowd. Usually, there is one player in particular they've come to see—Curry—and there is a common trait among those in the group. They are often children. Curry has the top-selling jersey in the NBA, and that is driven by the kids who flock to him.

"You see so many little kids with Steph jerseys begging for his autograph," Warriors coach Steve Kerr said. "They all identify with him."

Curry is aware of the effect famous athletes and mentors can have on kids when they meet them, whether positive or negative:

"My dad's teammates or the people he played against, if I sat in the hallway and I said 'Hey' and said 'What's up' to them, if they even said something back to me, that made my day. If they just cold-shouldered me, that hurt. It wasn't a lasting effect, but in the moment, that means a lot."

He also saw, up close, how his father dealt with kids during his career, and even after. That had a lasting impact on him.

> *"I got to see how gracious [my dad] was with everybody that came up to him, talking to the kids that looked up to him, spending a moment with them, understanding how valuable that interaction was. He was so consistent . . . Never knew I would be in that situation."*

Now that he is in that situation, though, he follows suit. He stops to sign autographs for kids in the stands, he visits schools and hospitals, and he interacts with kids at his public events.

> *"For kids to come to our games and if they go out of their way to try to connect with me, I do feel a responsibility for the kids for sure because that might make or break their confidence or their spirit on that specific day. That's my only opportunity to impact them in person."*

FIND AND SHARE YOUR JOY

If anything stands out about Curry's approach to his profession, his teammates, and opponents, to his coaches and mentors, it's that he brings a measure of joy to as many interactions and as many moments as he can. He likely would have done that if he had been a lawyer, a school teacher, or a veterinarian— it seems to be a built-in feature of his personality—but it has a much wider impact because he is an international star. There's something about succeeding as part of a team that makes it even more fulfilling for him:

> *"We don't do anything alone and being connected to a community, whether that is teammates and your coaching staff or in any industry, who you go to work with every day, whether that is your family—be really intentional in finding the joy in the experience."*

He has always found happiness in basketball, even late in his career. He had some trying times—as a high schooler who could not attract

"I'VE ALWAYS HAD A KIND OF QUIET KILLER INSTINCT."

attention, as a second-year NBA player with a dodgy ankle, losing the 2016 NBA Finals—but one of his lasting legacies will be the joy he brought to the game:

"We're all on this Earth for a reason, that's to lift each other up, spread positivity and love. Sometimes you can do it with a conversation or a word or a work of art; sometimes it is just how you carry yourself and how you live your life."

As nice as Curry can be in his personal life, nobody is just one thing. Don't expect him to be anything but a beast when he steps out onto the court: "I can have fun and have joy," explains Curry. But when the whistle blows, despite the smile that might be on his face, he remembers everyone who ever doubted him, he fires up that irrational confidence, and he gets straight to work destroying his opponents: "I'm out there to rip your heart out."

LIFE LESSONS FROM A LEGEND

- YOUR TIME IS YOUR BEST ASSET; BE WILLING TO GIVE IT.
- HELPING A CHILD CAN HAVE A LASTING IMPACT.
- LOOK FOR REASONS TO HAVE GRATITUDE, EVERY DAY.
- EVERYONE HAS THE POWER TO CHANGE SOMEONE ELSE'S LIFE.

"KEEP WORKING HARD.
EMBRACE THE
CHALLENGES
THAT YOU HAVE.
UNDERSTAND THAT
WE ALL HAVE GIFTS
FROM GOD THAT ARE
OUR PURPOSE IN LIFE."

FAITH, PASSION, AND THE DRIVE

"I've talked about faith, passion, and the drive with the guys that I've been around and the guys that surround me every single day. But a part of that is having the will to succeed. Knowing that you've put the work in and have the confidence to let it show. What I tell people is be the best version of yourself in anything that you do.

"You don't have to live anybody else's story. Sometimes people make it seem like you have to have certain prerequisites or a crazy life story in order to be successful in this world. But the truth is you really don't. It doesn't matter where you come from, what you have or don't have, what you lack or what you have too much of, but all you need to have is faith in God, an undying passion for what you do and what you choose to do in this life, and a relentless drive and the will to do whatever it takes to be successful in whatever you put your mind to.

"Make sure you live in the moment and work your butt off every single day, and I hope I inspire people all around the world to just be themselves, be humble, and be grateful for all the blessings in your life."

—STEPHEN CURRY, acceptance speech for the 2014–15 NBA MVP award, May 4, 2015

RESOURCES

PODCASTS/INTERVIEWS/ VIDEO CONTENT

"Doubted"
Nefarious Mini-Movie
January 12, 2021

"The Humble Giant"
Point Forward Podcast
March 9, 2022

"Lead by Example: 4-Time
NBA Champion Steph Curry
Sits Down with Warriors
President Bob Myers"
ESPN Video, January 17, 2023

"Steph Curry"
 The Draymond Green Show
April 14, 2022

"Steph Curry Joins Q and D"
The Knuckleheads Podcast,
February 16, 2022

"Stephen Curry"
All the Smoke Podcast
Episode 3, Season 2,
November 18, 2021

"Stephen Curry"
ASAP Sports Transcripts,
various dates

"Stephen Curry: 2X MVP & 3X NBA
Champion, Golden State Warriors"
*Stanford Graduate School of
Business Podcast,* June 10, 2020

"Stephen Curry Explains How He
Became the Greatest Shooter of
All Time"
The Konnor Mac Show, June 26, 2021

"Stephen Curry on Building the
Warriors Culture, Battling LeBron &
Kyrie, Changing the NBA & More"
The Old Man & the Three Podcast,
Episode 135, November 22, 2022

"Steph Curry on Creating
Winning Teams"
LinkedIn.com, March 20, 2017

"Stephen Curry Teaches Shooting,
Ball-Handling, and Scoring"
Stephen Curry, Master Class series

MAGAZINES/WEBSITES/ NEWSPAPERS

"After Offseason Focused on
Perfection, Stephen Curry Could
Be Even More Unstoppable"
NBA.com, October 22, 2021

"The Art and the Science: How
Stephen Curry Became the NBA's
3-Point King"
The Athletic, December 9, 2021

"The Birth of Steph"
The Ringer, March 14, 2018

"The Conflict Within Stephen
Curry: Raging Confidence and a
'Quiet Insecurity'"
The Athletic, October 7, 2021

"Curry, Calm and Collected"
The Ringer, February 16, 2022

"Drafting Stephen Curry: How
the Warriors Changed Forever
10 Years Ago"
San Francisco Chronicle,
June 25, 2019

"The Game That Changed Steph
Curry's Life"
Esquire, January 6, 2023

"The Home Team: Stephen Curry '10
on the Improbable Journey That
Began at Davidson"
Davidson.edu, December 1, 2022

"How Steph Curry Leads Like No
Other NBA Superstar"
ESPN.com, February 28, 2018

"How Stephen Curry Became the
NBA's Best Player"
GQ, November 19, 2015

"In 2009, Stephen Curry Had NBA
Draft Destination in Mind, and It
Wasn't Golden State"
Charlotte Observer, June 19, 2018

"Inside the Relationship that Unleashed Steph Curry's Greatness"
ESPN.com, May 17, 2019

"A Look at Stephen Curry's Humble Nature"
NBA.com, May 28, 2017

Stephen Curry
Instagram (@stephencurry30)

Stephen Curry
Twitter(@StephenCurry30)

"Steph Curry: 'My Next Move'"
The-Cauldron.com, March 26, 2015

"Stephen Curry, Ayesha Curry Continue to Make a Lasting Impact on Oakland's Kids"
Andscape, September 13, 2022

"Stephen Curry Doing More Than Just Shoot in Pursuit of Ring No. 4"
NBA.com, February 16, 2022

"Stephen Curry: 'It's Comical That People [Are] Saying I'm Having a Down Year'"
Bleacher Report, April 4, 2017

"Stephen Curry May Be the Best-Conditioned Player in the NBA, and His Incredibly Demanding Workouts Show Why"
Insider.com, June 10, 2022

"Stephen Curry Shares Best Advice Kobe Bryant Has Given Him"
SI.com, February 3, 2016

"Stephen Curry: The Full Circle"
ESPN Magazine, April 23, 2015

"Trust, Commitment, Care: A Coach, a Player and an Unbreakable Bond"
Davidson.edu, November 29, 2022

"Underrated"
The Players Tribune, January 9, 2019

BOOKS

Golden: The Miraculous Rise of Steph Curry, by Marcus Thompson

Golden Age: The Brilliance of the 2018 Champion Golden State Warriors, by Thomas Bevilacqua

Golden Days: West's Lakers, Steph's Warriors, and the California Dreamers Who Reinvented Basketball, by Jack McCallum

Golden Revival: A Dynastic Reunion and a New Generation Spark Warriors' Fourth Title in Eight Seasons, from the *San Francisco Chronicle*

The History of the NBA in 12 Games: From 24 Seconds to 30,000 3-Pointers, by Sean Deveney

I Have a Superpower, by Stephen Curry, Kevin R. Free, et al.

NBA Champions: Golden State Warriors, by Michael E. Goodman

Stephen Curry: I Know This to Be True, by Geoff Blackwell and Ruth Hobday

The Victory Machine: The Making and Unmaking of the Warriors Dynasty, by Ethan Sherwood Strauss

STATISTICAL WEBSITES

"Stephen Curry"
Basketball-Reference.com

"Stephen Curry"
NBA.com

"Stephen Curry"
stathead.com

"Stephen Curry"
Statmuse.com

"Stephen Curry"
Usab.com